Info Graphics for Educators

A Practical Guide for Teaching English Spelling

Scott Mills

Special Thank You: Gina Cooke, Doug Harper, Rebecca Marsh

LIV(E)

© 2018 Scott Mills

All Rights Reserved.

Introduction:

paradigm: an example or pattern of something.

A **paradigm** is defined as an example or pattern of something, or the underlying theories and methodologies of a particular scientific subject. In literacy education, the paradigm seems to be a pendulum that swings from whole language on one side to phonics on the other, never seemingly in the middle. Balanced literacy was supposed to be the great equalizer, but the curriculum pendulum nevertheless keeps swinging one way or the other.

Neither phonics nor whole language is informed about the differences between spoken language and written language, and neither is addressing the still approximately 40% of illiterate children nationwide.

If we continue in the current paradigm, where can we reasonably expect to see growth in our students? Can the paradigm shift?

This book is a collection of informational graphics grounded in principles that guide scientists and linguists in their professional endeavors. The scientific method begins with a hypothesis; so too should our approach to language.

orthography: a conventional writing system specific to one language that represents sense and meaning.

The graphics are not based on education research. Instead, they provide evidence from written language for the reader to explore, with suggestions to continue studying by revisiting the graphics. The accompanying glossary provides definitions from the field of **orthographic** linguistics designed to help the reader understand the vocabulary as it is presented within the text. Term definitions also aid in interpreting the matrices, charts, and diagrams contained within the graphics.

The purpose of the graphics is to provide visual information of how English orthography works. It is an effort to help others develop understanding descriptively. Because I am an educator, I have included notes with examples of how I have incorporated the science of linguistics into my day to day classroom instruction.

This book is not meant to be a curriculum, a scope and sequence, or a collection of handouts. If glanced at or skimmed, the information would probably be of little use. However, when studied thoroughly, the concepts presented reveal fascinating structures that exist within English. Therefore, the information is meant to be revisited again and again.

*A note on conventions: <> indicate spellings with letters to be named, / / enclose phonemes, and [ ] enclose phones where applicable.

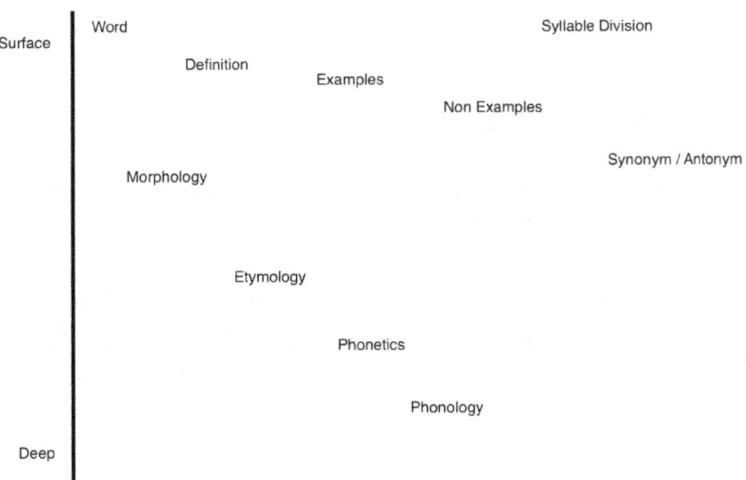

figure 1.1

awareness: a word attached to linguistic terms that doesn't apply to the scientific study of linguistics.

phonology: the study of units of speech that construct meaning.

phoneme: an abstract, minimal, distinctive, psychological unit that is represented by a written grapheme.

morphology: the study of the structure of words and word parts (bases and affixes) that contribute to meaning and/or syntax.

etymology: the study of the interrelationship between history and meaning of words.

Figure 1.1 is an approximate diagram to show that in the current education paradigm, there is a tendency to only focus on the surface levels of written language, but beautiful discoveries lie waiting deep below the surface.

In the current paradigm, the assumption is to start building what education researchers have termed "phonological **awareness**," but from the diagram we see that **phonology** is a deep structure. It lies well below the surface. We cannot understand phonology and associate **phonemes** with a written word until we have analyzed the structure and history of the word in question. Isolating a phoneme without context is not possible.

The graphics presented in this book suggest a shift in the current paradigm. It is time to break out of the pendulum swing, move beyond whole language and phonics, and explore the deep internal structures that exist within English orthography.

The assumptions I make throughout the book are that English writing operates in a hierarchical framework. Writing is, in fact, human *thought* made visible (Real Spelling).

Figure 1.2 represents a framework used to inform the graphics in the book.

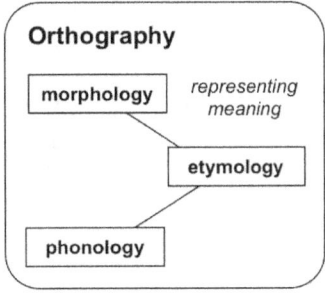

figure 1.2

Morphology:

Before studying the graphics, it is important to understand some specific terminology.

Written **morphemes**, or elements, can be subcategorized. Every word must have a base element, whether free or bound. That base element can join to affixes, connecting vowel letters, or other base elements to create compound words. Affixes, by definition, are bound.

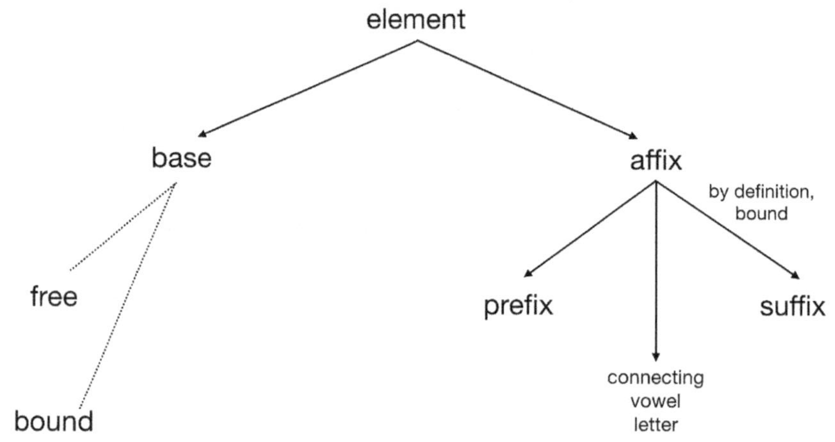

morpheme: minimal, psychological, distinctive unit of grammar. Smallest functioning unit.

base element: morpheme, free or bound, that carries the central meaning of a word.

free base element: a base element (e.g. graph) that is a word.

bound base element: a base element (e.g. -ject-) that attaches to other elements to form a word.

compound: a word containing more than one base element.

affix: an element that attaches, or joins to, a base element.

prefix: an affix that joins before a base element or to another prefix.

suffix: an affix that joins after a base element or to another suffix.

connecting vowel letter: an element that connects one element (base or affix) to another element.

denotation: the literal, often historical, sense and meaning of an element.

figure 2.1

If we apply these terms to analyze a lexical matrix, we can better understand the structure, or morphology, of words:

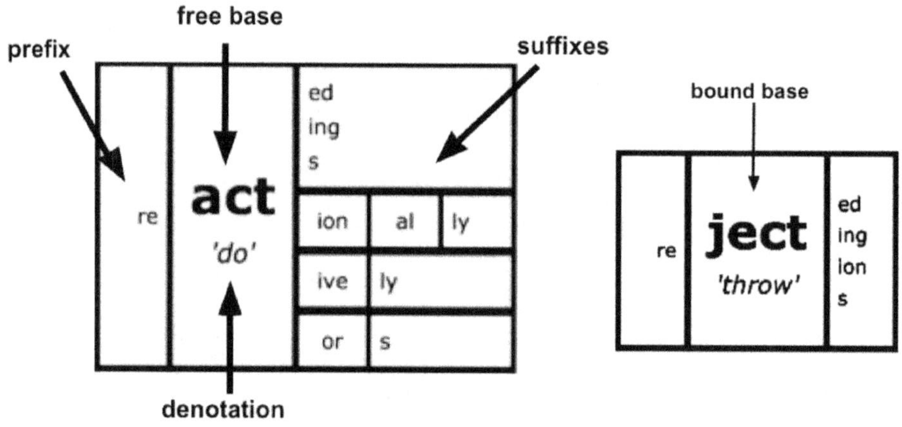

figure 2.2

A lexical algorithm, or word sum, can reveal the internal structure of a word:

synthesis: the process of putting together words with constituent morphemes.

- re + act + ed -> reacted
- re + act + ing -> reacting
- act + ion -> action

analysis: the process of analyzing words into morphemes.

- reacted -> re + act + ed
- reacting -> re + act + ing
- action -> act + ion

Notice that we can start with morphemes and synthesize, or put together, words in a process called **synthesis**, or we can start with words and analyze them into morphemes in a process called **analysis**.

lexeme: the fundamental unit of the lexicon of a language. *(e.g. walk, walks, walking are all forms of the English lexeme walk).*

In order for a suffix to be considered a morpheme, it must surface in other words and there must be etymological evidence for its existence. Affixes carry sense and meaning, but the central meaning of a word (**lexeme**) is contained within the base element.

Also contained within the graphics is the assumption of familiarity with spelling conventions as they are applied. There are three suffixing conventions in English which I have provided visuals for on the following pages.

Suffixing Convention #1

Consonant Doubling

Criteria

1) the suffix has an initial vowel letter
2) there is only one consonant letter in the final position in the base
3) there is just one vowel letter preceding that final consonant letter

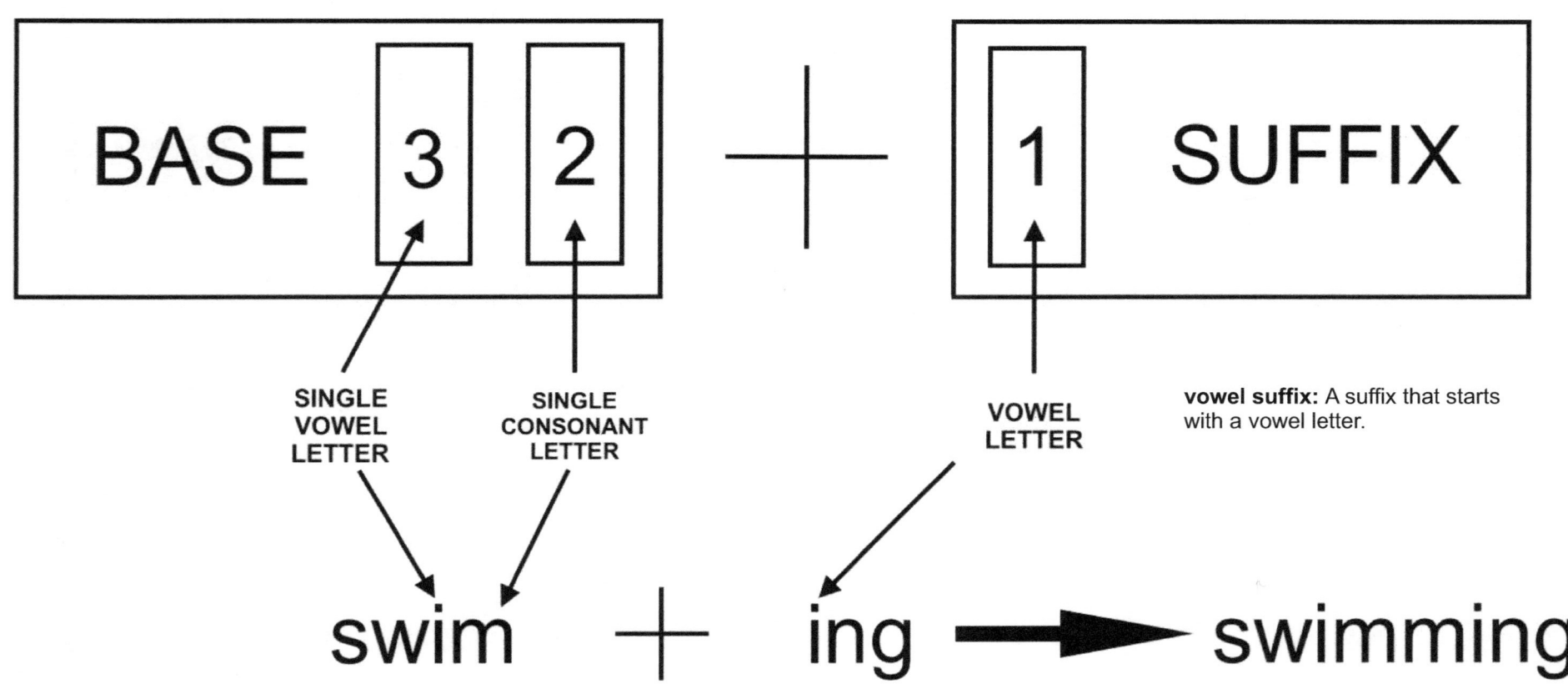

Suffixing Convention #2

Change \<y\> to \<i\> UNLESS:

1) the \<y\> is part of a digraph: \<ay\>, \<ey\>, \<oy\>, \<uy\>
2) the final synthesis will include a double \<i\>
3) the elements are forming a compound word

1

happy + ly → happily
plenty + ful → plentiful
lazy + ly → lazily

play + ful → playful
key + ed → keyed

2

cry + es → cries
cry + ed → cried
cry + ing → crying

fly + es → flies
fly + ing → flying

3

happy + ly → happily
plenty + ful → plentiful
lazy + ly → lazily

any + thing → anything
hay + wire → haywire

single, final, non-syllabic <e>:
Has multiple functions depending on where it surfaces. It may have more than one function in a single word.

Suffixing Convention #3

Replace a single, final, non-syllabic <e>:

If the base element has a single, final, non-syllabic <e>, then a vowel suffix will replace it.

A vowel suffix is a suffix that has an initial vowel letter: <-ed>, <-ing>, <-y>…(in suffixing, the <-y> usually acts as a vowel).

love + ly → lovely	care + ful → careful	create/ + ing → creating
love/ + ing → loving	care/ + ing → caring	create/ + ed → created
love/ + ed → loved	care/ + ed → cared	create/ + ion → creation

Notes for educators on morphology:

There are many possibilities for studying the three suffixing conventions. Some examples of these are:

- Vowel suffix review: One student (or the teacher) writes a suffix on the board and other students can walk around the room with a whiteboard and write "yes" or "no" depending on what type of suffix it is. This is a quick 5-minute review.

- Sorting vowel suffixes in "yes / no", or "vowel suffix / consonant suffix," columns. A consonant suffix would be one that did not start with a vowel.

- Using sentence stems, or clozed stems: "<-ed> is a vowel suffix because it starts with a vowel." "_____ is/is not a vowel suffix because _____."

- Adding or pasting prefixes and suffixes in their appropriate place(s) within a matrix that includes on the base element. Using the same morphemes to create new words, as in <re> + <act> + <s> -> reacts:

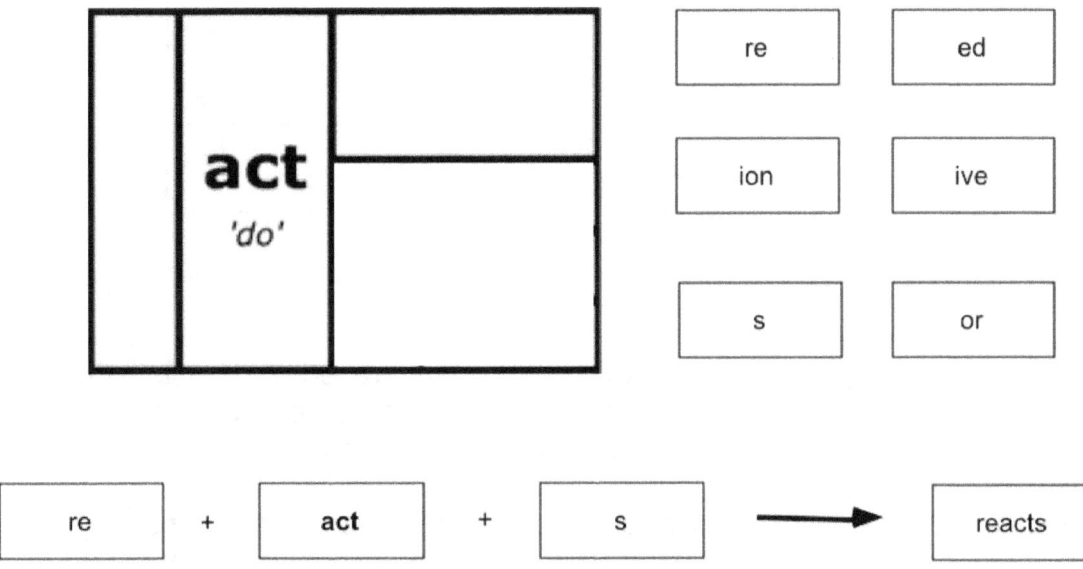

figure 3.1

The matrix is generative for deepening understanding of how morphemes join to create words.

Etymology

etymology: interrelation of history and meaning.

The denotation of the word *etymology* is "the study of the true sense of a word" (etymonline). In order to know that true sense, we have to look to the history and origin of a word, its **roots**. In other words, where did the word come from and how did it surface in English?

root: the historic origin of a PDE word. A root is not the same as a PDE base or lexeme. One root can be the source of several PDE words.

The historical context of how a word came to be in English is often overlooked, but it is a critical piece of the framework in order to understand why a word is spelled the way it is.

When tracing the etymology of a word, base, or element, I use diagrams that utilize approximate timelines, starting from earlier dates and moving toward Present-Day English (PDE) in an upward direction:

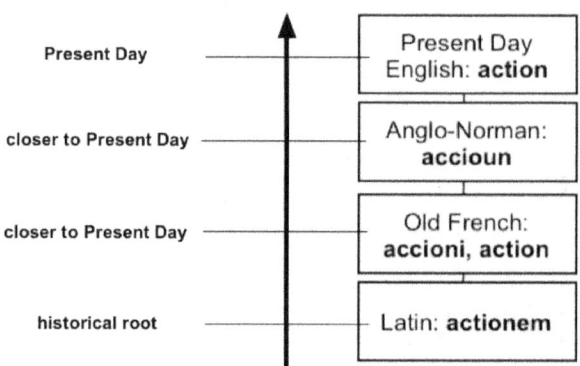

figure 4.1

diachronic: literally, "through time." Analyzing a word diachronically helps to determine its current spelling. It does not reveal the structure of PDE words, but can help account for that structure.

In figure 4.1, the lexeme action was traced back to its **root**, *actionem,* a Latin word that evolved through Old French and Anglo-Norman before surfacing in PDE as *action*.

Often, etymology can account for where an element comes from. However, it is important to note that etymology accounts for a **diachronic** relationship between words. Morphology, on the other hand, is **synchronic**. When working diachronically, we are going back in history, whereas with morphology, we are focused on the words we currently have in PDE. I use vertical lines and arrows to represent diachronic relationships and horizontal lines and arrows (e.g. in a word sum) to represent synchronic relationships.

synchronic: literally, "together with time." Analyzing words synchronically reveals the structure of PDE words.

Notes for educators on etymology:

Some examples for studying etymology in the classroom are:

- Color coding a chart using entries from the Online Etymology Dictionary (www.etymonline.com) and a diagram (figure 5.1).

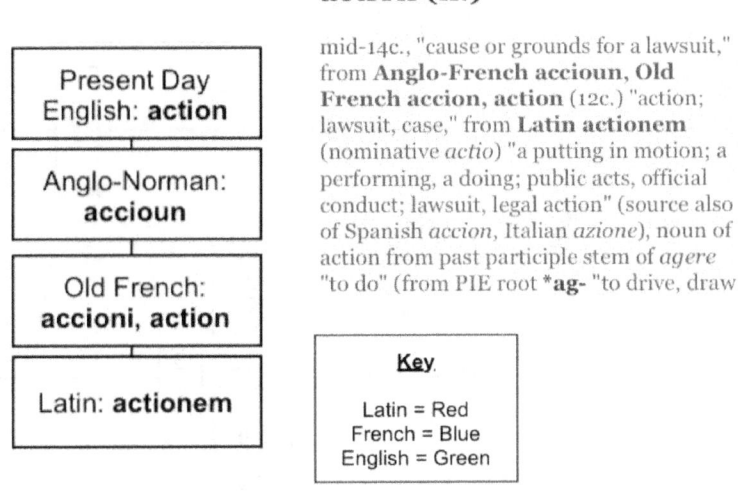

figure 5.1

- Students create their own etymology diagrams. The diagrams will eventually start to grow as students discover more words in PDE are derived from the same root (figure 5.2).

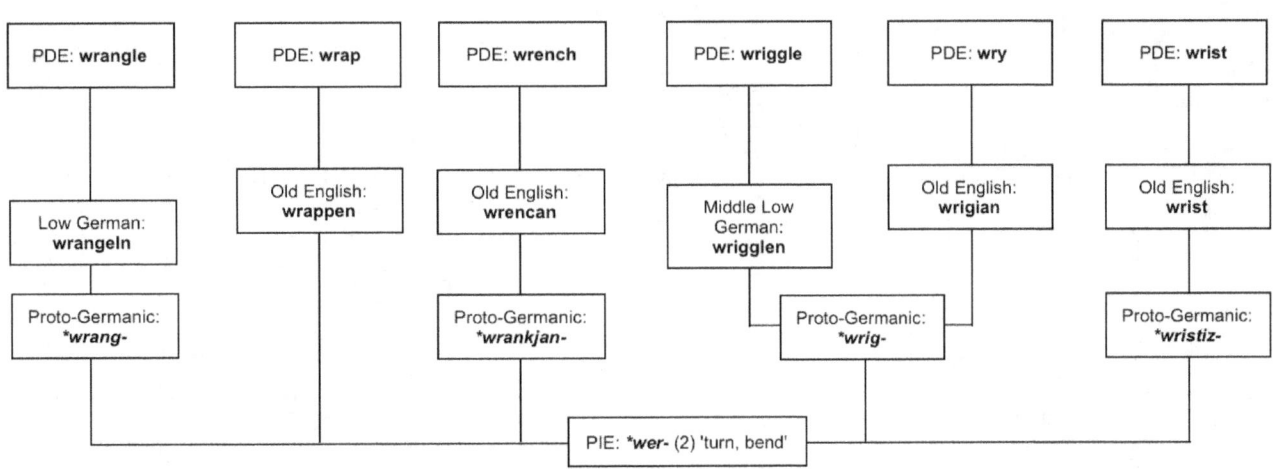

figure 5.2

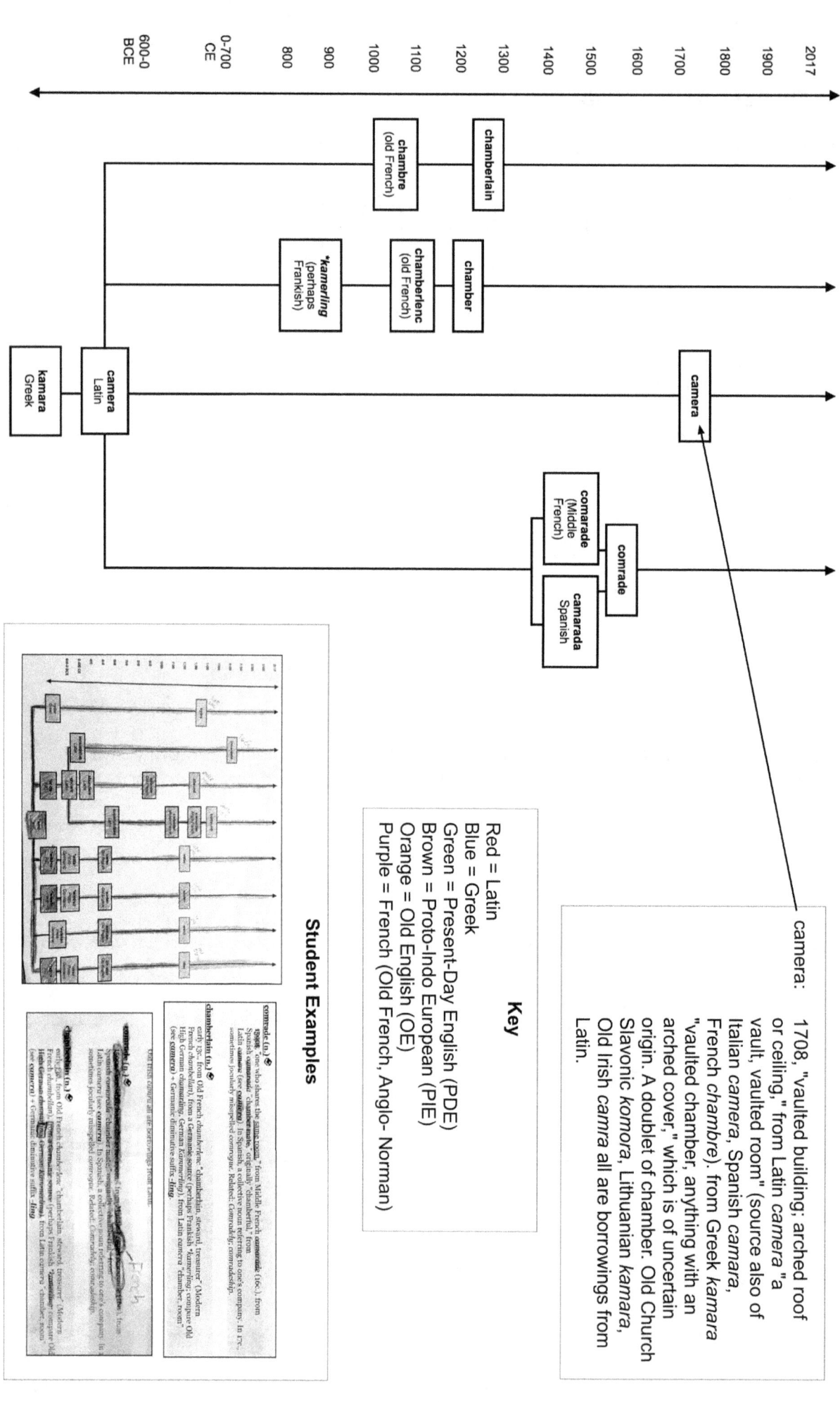

Phonology

Within literacy communities across the country, the overemphasis on "sound" is incredibly problematic. Encouraging a child to "sound out" some words (but not others) creates confusion for the student that is already having difficulty making sense of our orthography. Definitions of "phoneme" in education texts minimalizes the complexity when explaining to students that spelling and pronunciation don't always match. By suggesting that a word is a "sight word" when it does not have one-to-one grapheme-phoneme correspondence, or that a word is an "exception" when it doesn't follow a previously taught "rule" perpetuates student struggles.

Instead of suggesting students *sound it out* or *guess what word might make sense*, or an overreliance on picture cues for young readers, a powerful pedagogical change in verbal cuing will encourage students to focus on structure. Suggest the student spell out the word, or ask if they recognize any affixes or a base element.

Consider common words, often mislabeled as "sight words" despite the fact that their spelling is ordinary and explainable: *one*, *two*, *doubt*, *they*, *the*, and *of*. The rational for the spelling of these words lies in their history and their grammar, and can be explained to any school-aged child.

The following graphic shows a relationship between graphemes and phonemes that is clearly driven by meaning and context within the orthographic framework used throughout the book. By teaching within this framework, we can introduce students to how phonology is guided by morphology and etymology, rather than reinforcing English spelling as a random system of unexplained exceptions.

Two example student questions are followed through with explanations that involve analysis of:

1. meaning
2. morphology
3. etymology
4. grapheme-phoneme relationships

Only after analyzing the morphology and etymology of a word should phonology be considered.

Grapheme-Phoneme Correspondences

```
phoneme  ------------------------------→  /eɪ/
                                            ↑
grapheme ----→  <ay>    <ey>    <a>        
                 ↓       ↓       ↓         
lexeme          play    they    baby       
                day     prey    able       
                clay    obey    crazy      
```

When analyzing grapheme-phoneme correspondences, we can see that a phoneme might be represented by multiple graphemes.

The only possible way to account for a spelling is to look at structure and history. Here are two examples of student questions explained through investigations involving grapheme choice.

Why is there an <ey> digraph instead of an <ay> digraph surfacing word final in the lexeme *they*?

they

1. *they*: third person plural pronoun.

2. free base:
   they -> they

3. they, them, their

4. <ey> -> /eɪ/

If we only look at the surface, phonology-first approach, *they* would appear to be a word needing to be memorized, an exception to a rule. However, when we analyze the word's structure and history, we see the connection it bears to *them* and *their*. Those connections guide the spelling toward an <ey> digraph, rather than an <ay> digraph.

Why is *pray* spelled with an <ay> and *prey* spelled with an <ey>?

pray

1. *pray*: to request from a deity.

2. free base:
   pray -> pray

3. pray, praying, prayer

4. <ay> -> /eɪ/

prey

1. *prey*: animal that is hunted by another for food

2. free base:
   prey -> prey

3. preying, **predator**

4. <ey> -> /eɪ/

From this example we see that the word's meaning is the reason for the separate spellings. This is the homophone principle. Also notice the connection of *prey* to *predator*, connecting the <ey> digraph in *prey* to the <e> in predator.

It is important to note that teaching grapheme-phoneme correspondences can lead to the pitfall of isolating phonemes. It is not possible to account for spellings by isolating phonemes, as seen by the examples below. While a grapheme-phoneme correspondence chart can be a useful tool, it is the overarching framework of orthography that should guide spelling choices.

classroom example

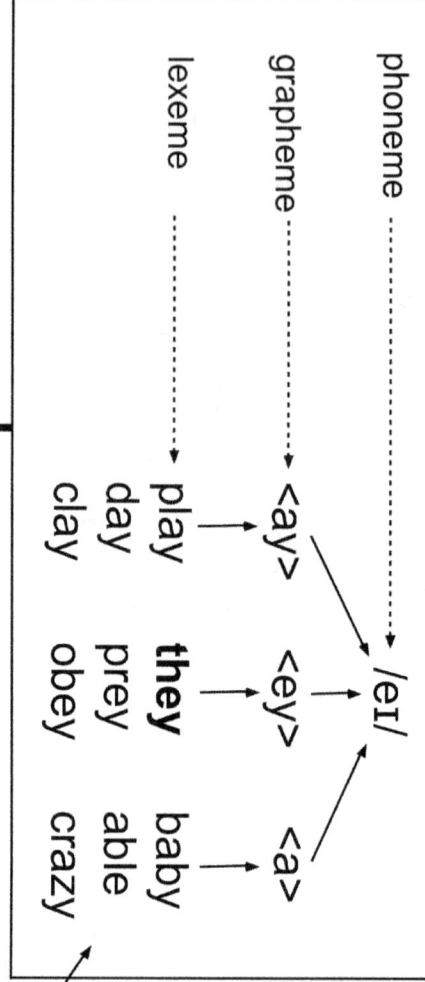

If we want to use the word *phonetic* to describe the English language, it's critical that we understand the terminology we choose. Phonetics is a branch of linguistics that involves the sounds of human speech. The symbols that represent phonetic notation are used in the International Phonetic Association (IPA). They represent not only the speech sounds from American English, but from all spoken languages. I incorporate the IPA in my classroom as a tool to reinforce the regularities in English spellings and assist non-native English speakers develop oral language.

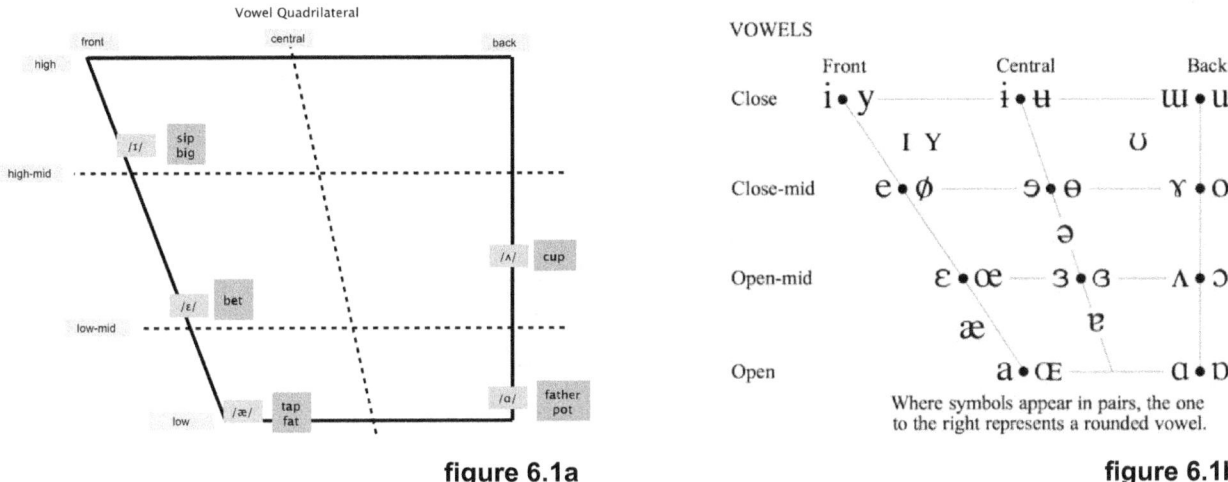

figure 6.1a   figure 6.1b

Figure 6.1a is an example vowel quadrilateral with accompanying words to provide context. Figure 6.1b is a more complete chart from the IPA. A vowel quadrilateral is the organization of vowels on a chart according to the shape the tongue takes in the mouth. It mirrors the structure of the mouth. When talking to students, I ask them to think about tongue placement in their mouths. Is the tongue body high, mid, or held lower in the mouth? Is it pushed forward or pulled back? Are the lips rounded or not? I ask them to consider what they are physically feeling.

When working with a consonant chart, figure 6.2a, I color code voiced/voiceless pairs of consonants and provide students with specific words that utilize those phonemes on Post-Its next to the symbols. They discuss place and manner of articulation, and they can see from the chart that a phoneme can be represented by several different graphemes. The chart is a visual and the Post-Its provide support in grapheme choice.

figure 6.2a   figure 6.2b

I don't refer to tools that represent the phonology of our language until my students have analyzed the morphology and etymology of a given word. Text is not the transcription of sound. There is more to consider when learning to spell.

Schwa:

schwa: a reduced, or neutral, vowel in an unstressed syllable.

A vowel quadrilateral is a useful visual for discussing the **schwa**.

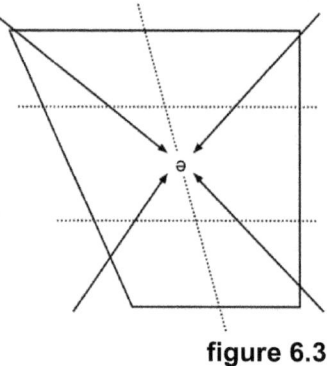

figure 6.3

A schwa makes sense in the context of a vowel quadrilateral, figure 6.3, as it is the most common vowel in English, and only occurs in unstressed **syllables**. It can be represented by any vowel grapheme. The placement in the mid-central space makes it easily identifiable visually, and in the context of other vowels.

Syllable:

English only has two types of syllables: open and closed. If a consonant coda is present, then the syllable is closed. If not, it is open. *Act* follows the pattern of a closed syllable: *v-c-c*. The prefix <pro-> in *produce* follows the open pattern: *c-c-v*.

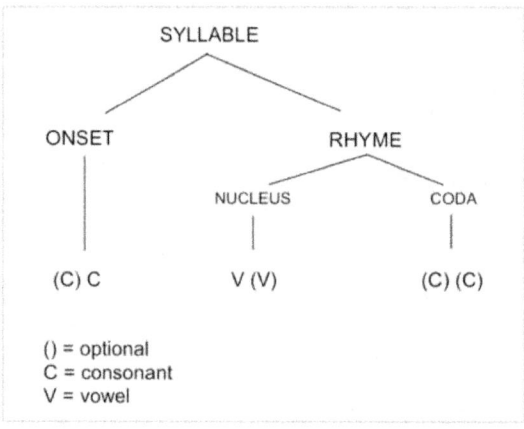

figure 6.4

Spending time analyzing syllables with students is counterproductive because it distracts from meaning and can obscure morphology. For example, a final <e> has several other functions than simply *marking a long vowel*. In some words, an <-le> serves as a suffix: *handle, amble*.

When contrasting syllables (surface forms) with the actual structure of each word, it is clear that syllable types are void of meaning and do not contribute to understanding English orthography.

Consider:

1. *ed - u - ca - tion* vs. *e + **duce**/ + ate/ + ion*
2. *mu - sic* vs. ***muse**/ + ic*
3. *spec - tac - u - lar* vs. ***spect** + ac + ule/ + ar*

The matrix, on the other hand, builds understanding of meaning connections between words and will only enhance a student's vocabulary and their ability to spell.

Stress:

stress: the degree of force used when producing a spoken syllable.

English is a stress-timed language, not a syllable-timed language, like Latin or Spanish. Introducing the concept of stress to students can be done through homographs, and simultaneously with the vowel quadrilateral. Although I've isolated the words in figure 6.5 and marked the stress to compare the words, placing a word in a phrase or sentence is essential to derive meaning.

Stress		
Noun	**Verb**	Without context, a word's stress cannot be determined. Using the word in a phrase or sentence will aid in understanding where the stress occurs and how stress affects meaning.
'object	ob'ject	
'affect	af'fect	
'produce	pro'duce	
'conflict	con'flict	
'incline	in'cline	
*stress marked with a '		Examples:
Even though the spelling remains consistent, changing the stress from the first syllable to the second syllable can change the word's grammar.		I objéct! The óbject is on the table. I pro'duce graphics. The 'produce is on the table.

figure 6.5

Introducing a concept:

When I introduce the terms from the orthography framework (figure 1.2) to students, I am explicit. I start with the element chart (figure 2.1) and make each student a blank copy of it. I write a simple concept statement on the board:

"Concept statement: An element is a unit of language that has meaning." I then have students write the concept in their notebook and repeat it with a partner. I am explicit. (move to the first sentence). I don't want my students to guess at what they "think" is an element. I just want them to know what it is, so I tell them.

I start with a free base. "A free base is an element that can stand alone as a word. Examples of free bases are *play*, *go*, and *do*. Class, what is a free base? Turn and talk to your partner. Talk to your group to verify. Partner A, what is a free base? What are some examples?" The discussion piece is extremely important. I want my students to verbalize the concepts, to solidify and practice discussing meaningful content, especially second language learners.

I then move to each part of the chart, each time having students write out student-friendly definitions of the terms and having them discuss and report out to the class with examples and non-examples. This goes on for a class period. We review constantly.

The routine of presenting a concept statement, followed by discussion and practice never changes because students know what to expect. They know they will be asked to discuss the terms and they know they will have to report out at some point.

The morphology basics are the same. We discuss and practice doing word sums every day. Sometimes we put up a matrix and just do the word sums until students are comfortable with them.

The suffixing convention basics are presented the same way, with the concept statement, the discussion and the practice.

In working within the confines of a school curriculum, connecting words with morphology, etymology and phonology can be done through vocabulary, station work and/or explicit lessons. Sometimes I select the words for students to study. Other times students will self-select words to investigate.

Further examples of activities integrating morphology and etymology used with students are included on the following pages.

Step 1:

explicitly teach words that share a base:

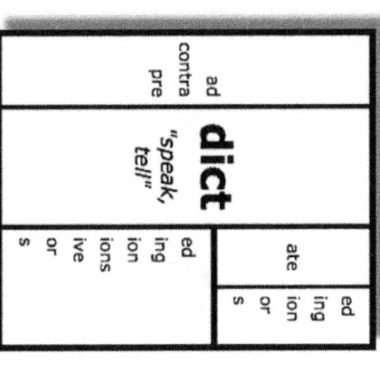

contradict
contra + dict

Denotation: (v) "speak against"
Example: As the men were arguing, they continued to **contradict** each other's statements.

addict
ad + dict

Denotation: (n) "to devote, give one's assent to"
Example: The girls were **addicted** to talking about clothes.
Pronunciation: /kəˈlætrəl/

predict
pre + dict

Denotation: (v) "tell before"
Example: The weatherman tried to **predict** rain for tomorrow in his forecast.
Pronunciation: /prəˈdɪkt/

Step 2:

Students use examples and create words to study:

Picture

What does it mean?
Sentence: _____.

How is it built?
Word Sums:

How is/are the word(s) pronounced?

*How does adding an <-ion> suffix change each of your constructions?

Bonus Questions lead to deeper investigations:

What does it mean?

What are the relatives?

WORD

How is it built?

What are the important parts of pronunciation?

What does it mean?

water falling down

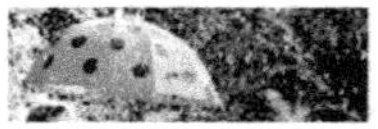

The rain fell down.
It was beginning to rain.
It is raining today.

What are the relatives?

Today: rain
Old English: regn
Germanic: *regna
PIE: *reg-

WORD
rain

How is it built?

rain -> _____ *free base
rain + s -> _____
rain + ing -> _____
rain + ed -> _____
rain + coat -> raincoat *compound

What are the important parts of pronunciation?

What do you feel when you pronounce the graphemes?

Minimal pairs:
Initial: pain, gain, main, chain
Medial:
Final: raid, rail

r	ai	n
ɹ	eɪ	n

Student Examples

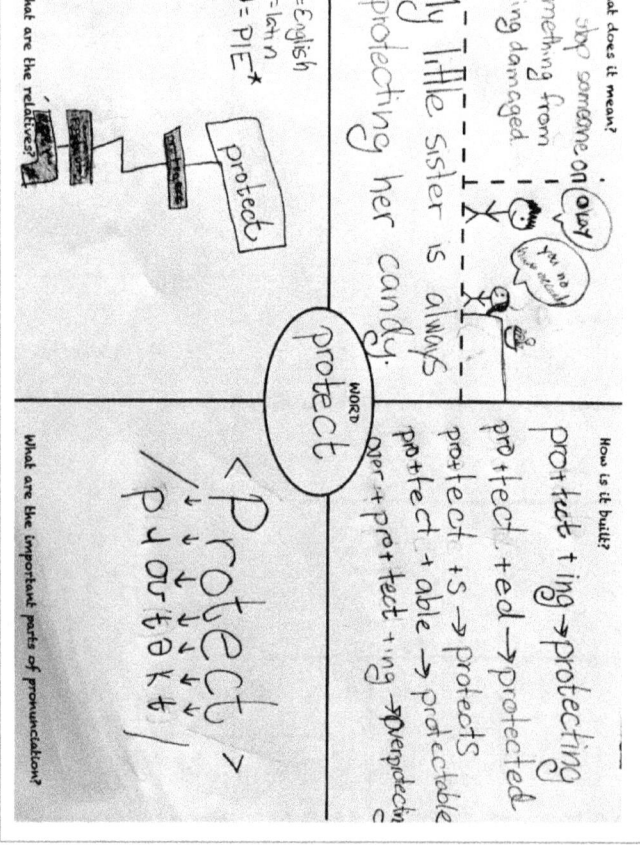

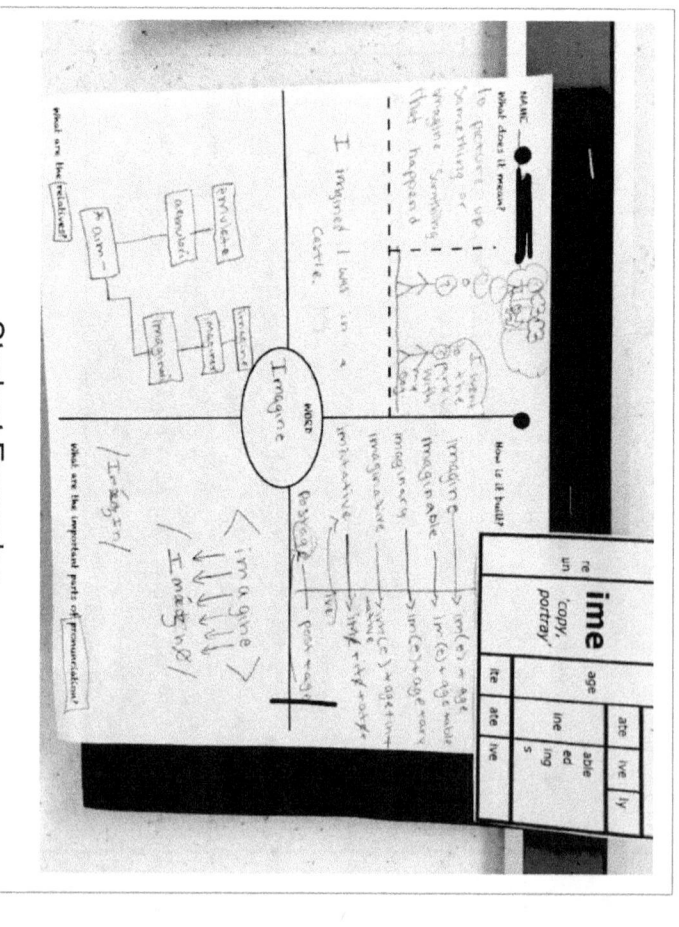

Word Sums

sub	com	**pact**	ed	s
	im	'fasten'	ing	
			ly	
			ness	

What is the PIE reconstructed root of the base element *pact*?

List eight English cognates of *impact*:

1.   5.
2.   6.
3.   7.
4.   8.

Student Examples

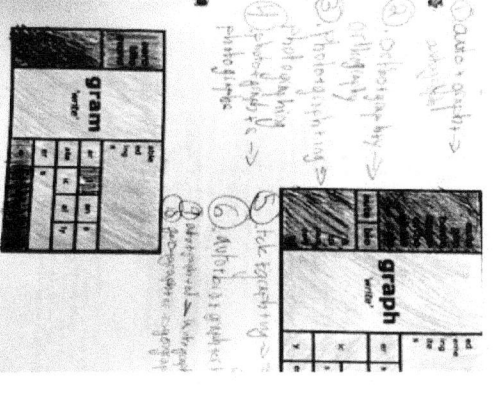

Integrating the Framework

The purpose of the preceding pages was to provide a framework for investigating words scientifically and comparatively. Since most schools have a literacy curriculum, informal assessments can help determine if students are able to show mastery of:

- analysis and synthesis of words using morphology
- using the lexical algorithm to represent analyses and syntheses
- using etymological resources to investigate word histories
- familiarity with the IPA

The information included in the following graphics was gathered by investigating words through the framework described in figure 1.2. The graphics are meant to be viewed side-by-side with the accompanying written explanation. None of the following pages are meant to be handouts or consumables for classroom use.

Is there a *<-tion> suffix?

The following graphic investigates the commonly held assumption that *<-tion> is a suffix. In analyzing the morphology, one hypothesis states that the word *action* can be analyzed: <ac> + <tion> with a *<-tion> suffix. In the second hypothesis, <act> + <ion>, it is clear the <t> is part of the base element, rather than the suffix. In comparing other English lexemes: *option, fiction, instruction, etc...* there is no evidence of a *<-tion> suffix that is valid. In every lexeme, the <t> is a part of the preceding base element, not the suffix.

Generalizing the concept also reveals evidence to falsify a *<-sion> suffix.

Consider:

fission -> fiss + ion (from Latin)

mission -> miss + ion (from Latin)

vision -> vise/ + ion (from Latin, via French)

action

meaning
n. the act or process of doing something

etymology
Present Day English: **action**
Anglo-Norman: **accioun**
Old French: **accioni, action**
Latin: **actionem**

morphology

hypothesis 1: ac + tion -> action

ac + tive -> active

*<ac> carries no meaning and *<-tive> is not a suffix.

But, <-ive> is a suffix that forms adjectives from verbs, usually derived from Latin <-ivus>. Examples include: cursive, elusive, passive, positive, and massive.

ac + t -> act

*<ac> carries no meaning.

<-t> is a Germanic suffix. There is no <-t> suffix in English that derives from Latin. Examples of the Germanic suffix <-t> include burnt, built and learnt.

ac + tor -> actor

There is no <-tor> suffix.

But, there is an <-or> suffix derived from Latin <-orem>. It creates nouns of quality, state or condition. The British equivalent spelling is <-our>. Compare: glamor ~ glamour, harbor ~ harbour, labor ~ labour

hypothesis 2: act + ion -> action

act + ive -> active

act + or -> actor

The elements (morphemes) in each of the word sums can be accounted for through their etymology and meaning.

	act 'do'		
re		ion	al	ly
		ive	ly	
		or	s	
		s		
		ed		
		ing		

phonology

a	c	t	i	o	n
æ	k	ʃ	Ø	ə	n

<t> ⎯⎯ /t/
    ⎯⎯ /ʃ/

What is the <wr> digraph?

A third concept conveyed in the following graphic invites the reader to ponder the consistencies that exist with the word initial <wr> digraph found in the initial position in bases of Germanic origin. These bases containing the initial <wr> digraph have a sense and meaning of bending, twisting, or turning.

I have provided a matrix with the free base *wrest*, which can be generative and used alongside word sums in a classroom, as well as an etymology diagram that leads back to Proto-Indo European (PIE). This is the first chart that uses an asterisk (*) to show that the root was not written, but reconstructed by linguists. Even though we have no written record of PIE roots, linguists have spent considerable time reconstructing them from evidence.

For further study, check etymonline.com for Latinate words that come from the same PIE reconstructed root *wer-. This can lead to exciting discoveries and generative conversations about the relationships between the letters <v>, <w>, and <u>.

<wr>

The <wr> digraph is word initial.

The <wr> digraph signals Germanic origin.

The <wr> digraph surfaces in words in Present Day English that have a sense of twisting or turning.

For further study:

Words deriving from the Latin root *vertere*.

The letters <v> and <w>, and their relationship to <u>.

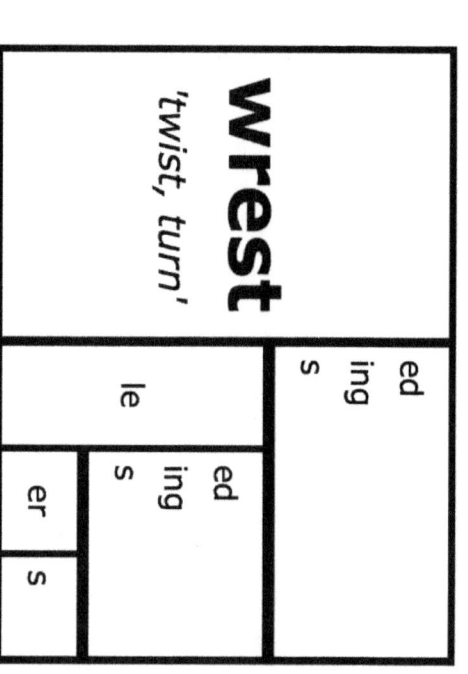

wrest *'twist, turn'* — ed, ing, s, le, s, ed, ing, er, s

PDE: **wrangle** — Low German: **wrangeln** — Proto-Germanic: **wrang-*

PDE: **wrap** — Old English: **wrappen**

PDE: **wrench** — Old English: **wrencan** — Proto-Germanic: **wrankjan-*

PDE: **wriggle** — Middle Low German: **wrigglen** — Proto-Germanic: **wrig-*

PDE: **wry** — Old English: **wrigian** — Proto-Germanic: **wrig-*

PDE: **wrist** — Old English: **wrist** — Proto-Germanic: **wristiz-*

PIE: **wer-* (2) 'turn, bend'

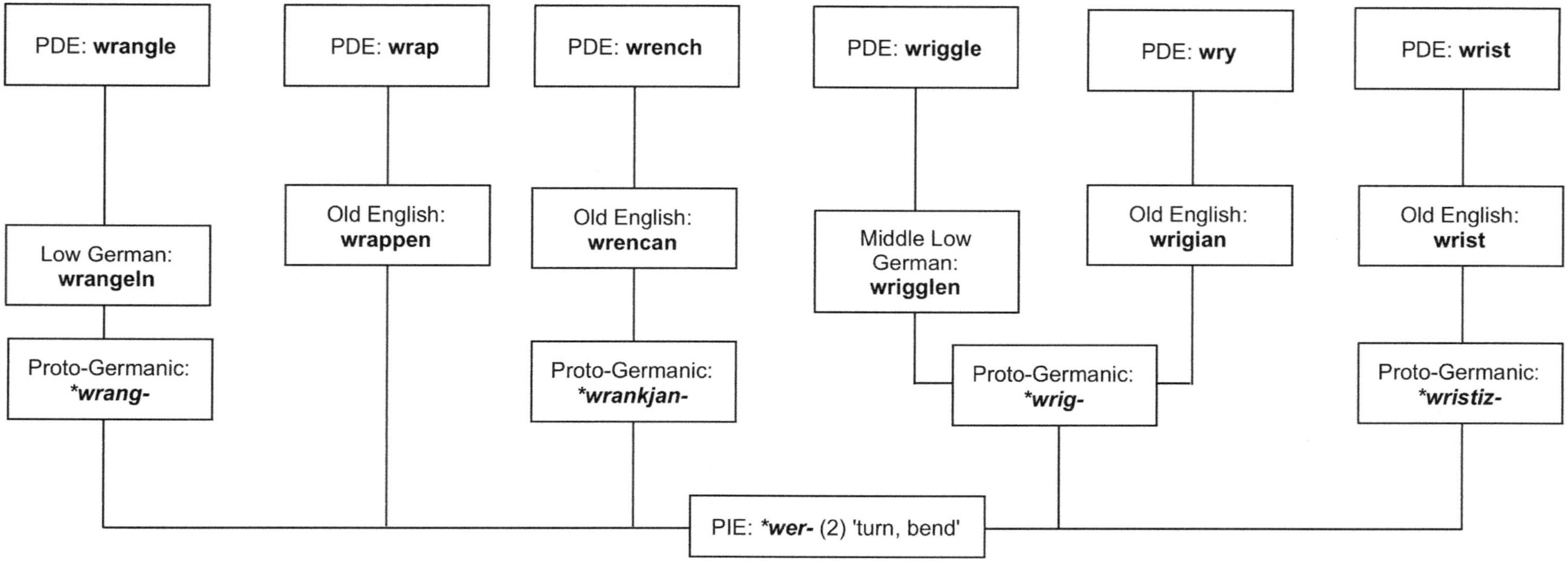

What is a cognate?

This graphic shows a side by side comparison of the evolution of two Latin roots: *gnoscere* and *gnasci*, which yield the homographic PDE bound base element <gn>. Through etymology, we can see that they are clearly distinct elements, even though they are spelled the same. This shows the importance of the historical context when analyzing words.

I have provided sample matrices for generative discussions and practice to help promote a better understanding of how morphemes interact. Etymology diagrams for a few PDE cognates are included as well.

For further study, look at sublexical units that are cognates, or cognate languages as a whole.

<gn>

The meanings of *recognize* and *cognate* can be thoroughly understood through their respective morphologies and etymologies. The belief that cognates are words that sound and/or look the same is an imprecise definition. Through the structure: co + gn + ate -> cognate, we can identify all the morphemes. The <co-> is an assimilated prefix of <com->, usually denoting 'with.' The base element <gn> derives from the Latin root *gnosci*, denoting 'born.' Finally, the <-ate> suffix forms a noun and derives from the Latin <-atus>. Two or more words can be cognates if they are "born with" each other, or derive from the same root. The evidence presented in this graphic shows two *homographic* base elements that have derived from Latin origins.

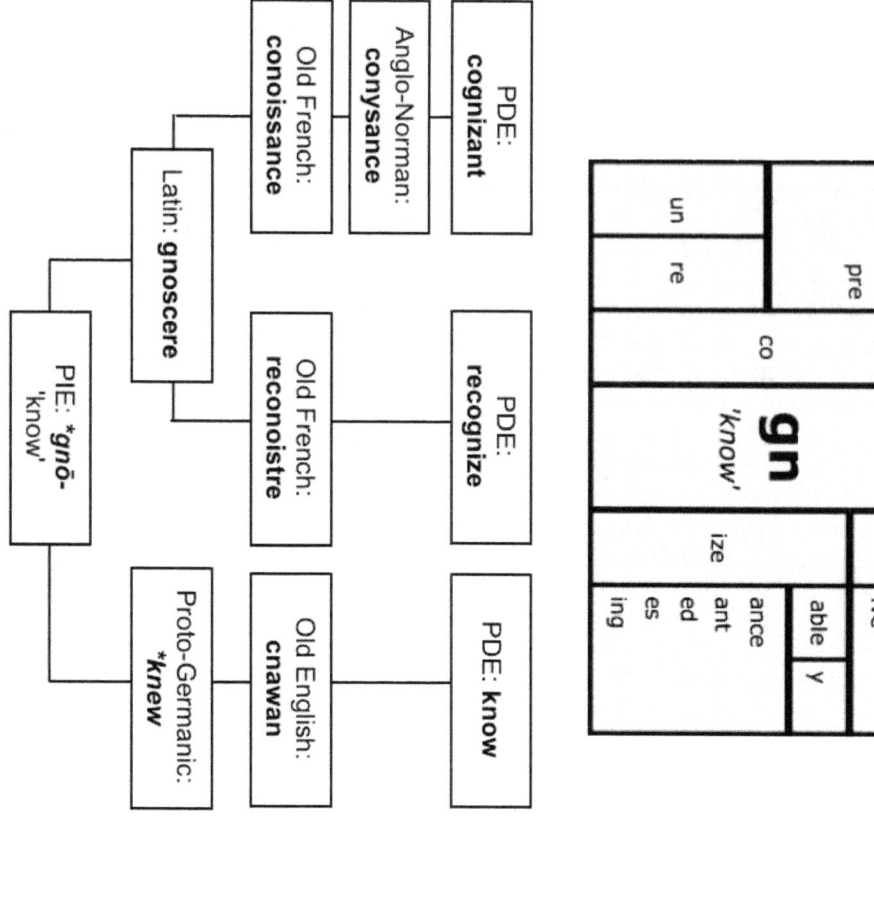

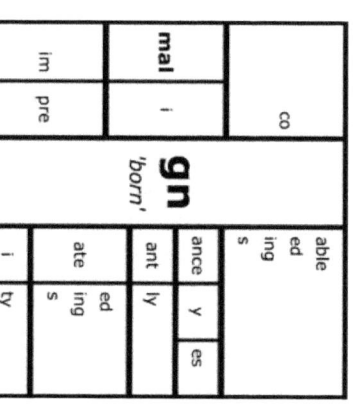

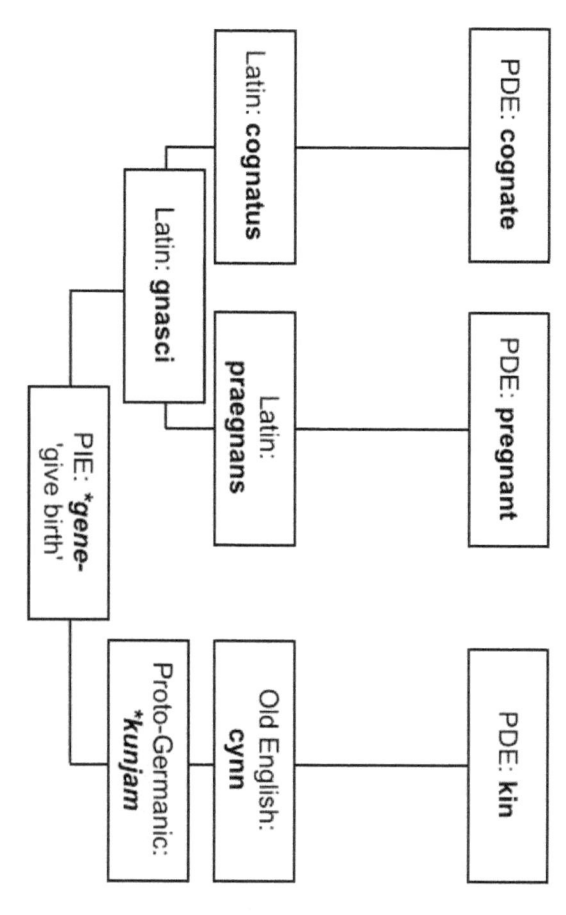

For further study:

What other cognates are derived from the PIE reconstructed roots **gene-* and **gnō-* ?

What languages are considered cognate?

Cognate suffixes <-ous> and <-ose>:

The following graphic compares word pairs in PDE that have a surface level spelling change, but that spelling change can be accounted for by analyzing the structure and etymology.

Noticing that the words in the left column function as adjectives (when in context!) and the words in the right column function as nouns (when in context!) is only part of the story.

We can use the lexical algorithm as shown in the next two boxes to identify a consistent base element, and then look for evidence of the suffixes.

The etymology diagram provides concrete evidence of the cognate suffixes <-ose> and <-ous>. The <-ity> suffix requires further inquiry.

adj.	curious	?	curiosity	n.
adj.	luminous	?	luminosity	n.
adj.	generous	?	generosity	n.
adj.	virtuous	?	virtuosity	n.
adj.	monstrous	?	monstrosity	n.
adj.	religious	?	religiosity	n.
adj.	porous	?	porosity	n.
adj.	pompous	?	pomposity	n.
adj.	verbose	?	verbosity	n.

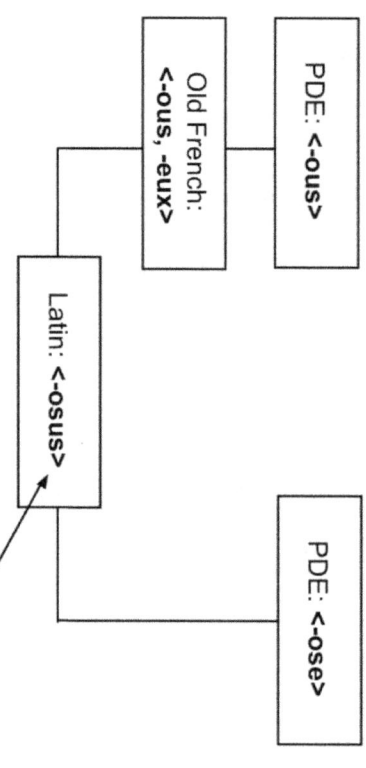

PDE: <-ous>
Old French: <-ous, -eux>
Latin: <-osus>
PDE: <-ose>

```
curious -> cure + i + ous
luminous -> lume + ine + ous
generous -> gene + er + ous
virtuous -> virtue + ous
monstrous -> monstr + ous
religious -> relig + i + ous
porous -> pore + ous
pompous -> pomp + ous
verbose -> verb + ose
```

```
curiosity -> cure + i + osity
luminosity -> lume + ine + osity
generosity -> gene + er + osity
virtuosity -> virtue + osity
monstrosity -> monstr + osity
religiosity -> relig + i + osity
porosity -> pore + osity
pomposity -> pomp + osity
verbosity -> verb + osity
```

The base element in each set of **algorithms** stays the same. It acts as a control variable and allows us to compare the suffixes.

We can look to see if <-osity> is simple, or if it contains more than one element, thereby rendering it complex:

lexity -> lex + ity
fatality -> fatal + ity
enormity -> enorm + ity

verbose -> verb + ose
verbosity -> verb + ose + ity

We have evidence of an <-ity>.

We can reasonably conclude: <osity> -> <ose> + <ity>

We also have etymological evidence further proving the relationship between the <-ous> and <-ose> suffixes.

We see <-ose> and <-ous> both form adjectives when we look at where these suffixes surface in other words.

For further study:

If the <-ose> suffix is not what is creating the nouns in the paradigm, what is? What is the <-ity>?

What is the <-ose> in *dextrose*, *glucose*, *sucrose* and *fructose*?

Comparing Spanish and English

As seen from the previous cognate graphic, listing cognates in a t-chart and labelling them as words that "sound the same" and "look the same" will perpetuate the identification of false cognates. Surface level instruction that excludes investigating etymology should be avoided.

The following patterns compare a few different English suffixes with their Spanish cognates. By comparing more than one language, deeper structures are revealed. Consider the following:

    open + **ly** -> openly   abierta + **mente** -> abiertamente

    rapid + **ly** -> rapidly   rápida + **mente** -> rápidamente

    furious + **ly** -> furiously   furiosa + **mente** -> furiosamente

    sad + **ly** -> sadly   triste + **mente** -> tristemente

    perfect + **ly** -> perfectly   perfecta + **mente** -> perfectamente

From the synthesis, we see that the <-ly> suffix is analogous to the <-mente> suffix in Spanish.

In addition, the etymology reveals that the <-ly> in these words is Germanic and denotes "body" and the Latin counterpart from which <-mente> derives denotes "mind."

Spanish Suffixes

<-y> : <-ia>

biography	:	biografía
victory	:	victoria
history	:	historia
hypocrisy	:	hipocresía
family	:	familia

When comparing words in English with a <-y> suffix that forms nouns (there are several homographic <-y> suffixes in English) with words in Spanish, we can discover a <-ia> suffix.

When looking for etymological evidence, we see that both derive from the Latin <-ia> suffix with the same function across both languages.

<-ly> : <-mente>

openly	:	abiertamente
rapidly	:	rápidamente
furiously	:	furiosamente
sadly	:	tristemente
perfectly	:	perfectamente

When comparing words in English with a <-ly> suffix that forms adverbs (there is another homographic <-ly> suffix in English) with words in Spanish, we can discover a <-mente> suffix.

When looking for etymological evidence, we see that the <-ly> suffix came from Germanic and originally denotes "body," whereas the Latinate form <mente> originally denotes 'mind.'

<-ty> : <-dad>

ability	:	capacidad
safety	:	seguridad
diversity	:	diversidad
unity	:	unidad
gravity	:	gravedad

When comparing words in English with a <-ty> suffix that forms abstract nouns (there is another homographic <-ty> suffix in English) with words in Spanish, we can discover a <-dad> suffix.

When looking for etymological evidence, we see that both are derived from Latin <-tatem>

For further study:

What other suffixes exist in Spanish?

Analyzing the Latin noun

While there are several cases of the Latin noun, for the purposes of English orthography, the Latin nominative and genitive cases are of particular interest.

In order to derive a PDE base element, it is often the inflectional suffixes removed from the genitive case.

When using a reference source, such as a Latin dictionary, the header entry is usually given with the nominative case. The Online Etymology Dictionary will often give both the nominative and genitive cases.

The cases fall into what are called declensions. There are five Latin noun declensions that have various suffixes, depending on the declension. Figure 7.1 is a reference for Latin inflectional suffixes according to declension and case.

Latin Inflectional Suffixes by Declension

declension	1	2	3	4	5
nominative	-a	-us, -er, -um	varies	-us, -u	-es
genitive	-ae	-i	-is	-ūs	-ei

figure 7.1

The following graphic is a step by step analysis of several Latin nouns.

Analyzing the Latin verb

The Latin verb has four principal parts, two of which account for how PDE derives its base elements. The following graphic delves deeper into word pairs and how they are derived from Latin.

The graphic is meant to be studied from the top left corner using the example Latin verb *suadere,* meaning 'suggest.' The PDE base elements are revealed after removing the Latin suffixes from the second and fourth principal parts of the verb. Since both elements are productive (PDE words are derived from both parts), we can refer to these elements as twin bases. Both elements are bound since neither is a word on its own when placed in context.

Notice that when analyzing the Latin verb *suadere*, we remove the Latin suffix <-ere>. This leaves the stem <suad->, but every base element that comes into English has a single, potential, non-syllabic, final <e> that may or may not realize that potentiality when synthesized using the lexical algorithm. In English, the word *persuade* is evidence that the potentiality of the <e> has been realized. The <e> surfaces word final. Suffixing convention #3 explores how the <e> is replaced in syntheses. The "grayed" out <e> in <suase> in the matrix serves to show its potential.

Finally, we can generalize this concept and look for patterns. While there is a pattern that shows the second principal part <-suade-> as forming what can eventually be used as a verb, the word *persuader,* with the <-er> suffix forming an agent noun, falsifies this hypothesis. Hence, in the graphic, the word *sometimes* is used to describe the pattern.

Analyzing the Latin noun:

declension		
case		
nominative	aqua	
genitive	aquae	

Step 1: Locate the nominative case in your reference.

Step 2: Locate the genitive case.

aquae → aqu-

Step 3: Remove the inflectional suffix. This will vary depending on what declension it falls under. There are five declensions.

Step 4: The result of the analysis is a productive base element.

Step 5: The base element can be synthesized. Note that the resulting base element can compound, sometimes with a connecting vowel letter, and can attach to affixes.

aqu + i + Fer -> aquifer
aqu + ary/i +um -> aquarium
aqu + ate/ + ic -> aquatic
aqu + e + Duct -> aqueduct

The resulting syntheses are Present-Day English derivations. All of these morphemes could be put into a generative matrix.

examples

servus, servī ⟶ servī- ⟶ serv- ⟶ serve

rex, rēgis ⟶ rēgis ⟶ reg- ⟶ reg e

cīvis, cīvis ⟶ cīvis ⟶ civ- ⟶ civ e

*Notice the resulting final, single non-syllabic <e> in each of the base elements. In serve the <e> surfaces, making it a free base element. Its potentiality is marked by the lighter shade in the bound bases <reg(e)> and <civ(e)>.

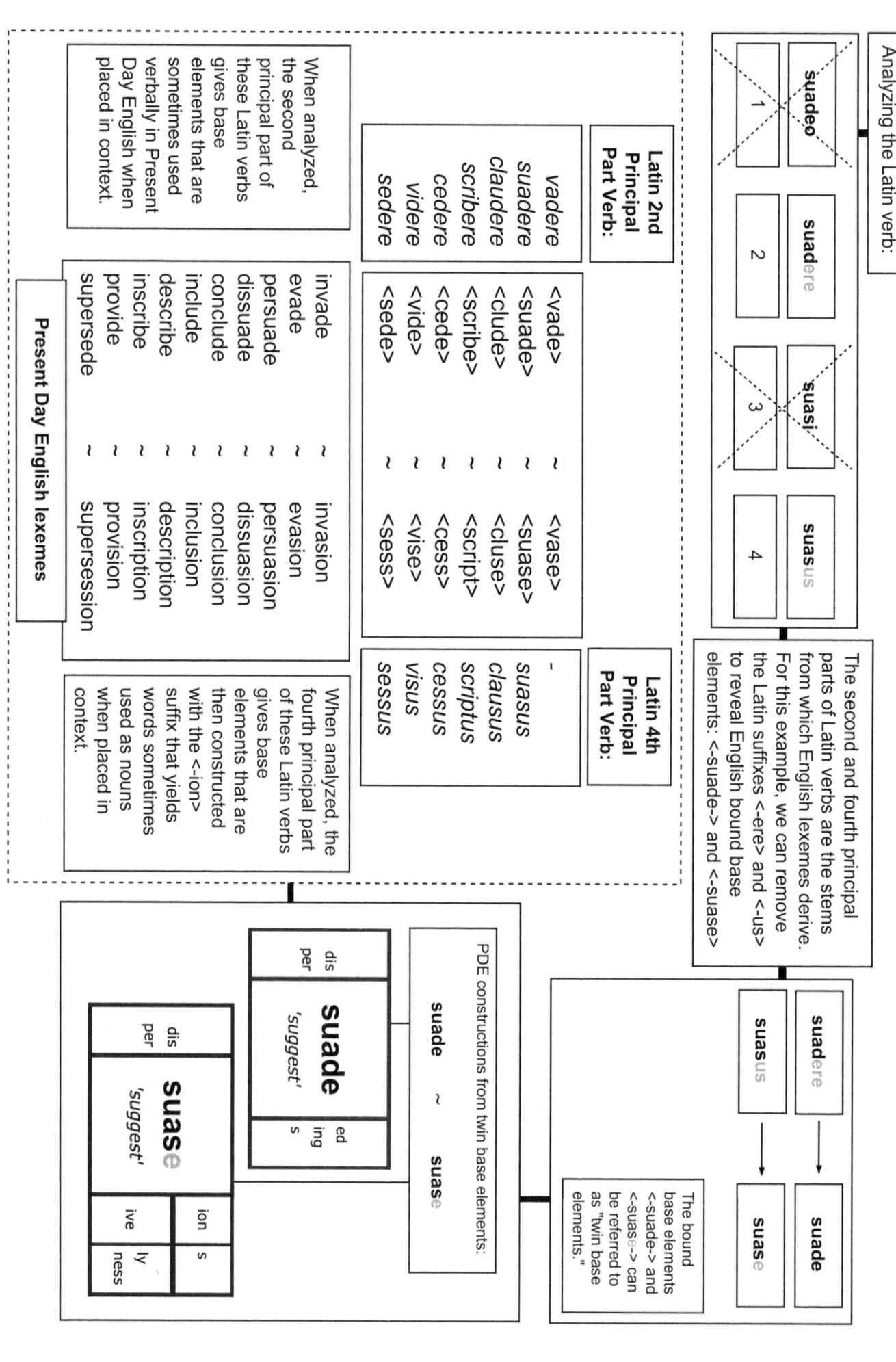

Lexical Doublets

A lexical doublet is a pair of English lexemes that derive from the same etymon. Certain rigorous criteria must be met in order for two lexemes to be considered lexical doublets:

- must derive from the same etymon
- must have similar, albeit slightly different meanings
- must have the same grammatical class (e.g. noun, adjective, verb)
- must have one evolutive and one punctual derivation, with the evolutive derivation entering English through a different pathway than the punctual derivation
- must be two distinct written forms (spellings)

Figure 8.1 provides more information to help the reader understand the next three example charts.

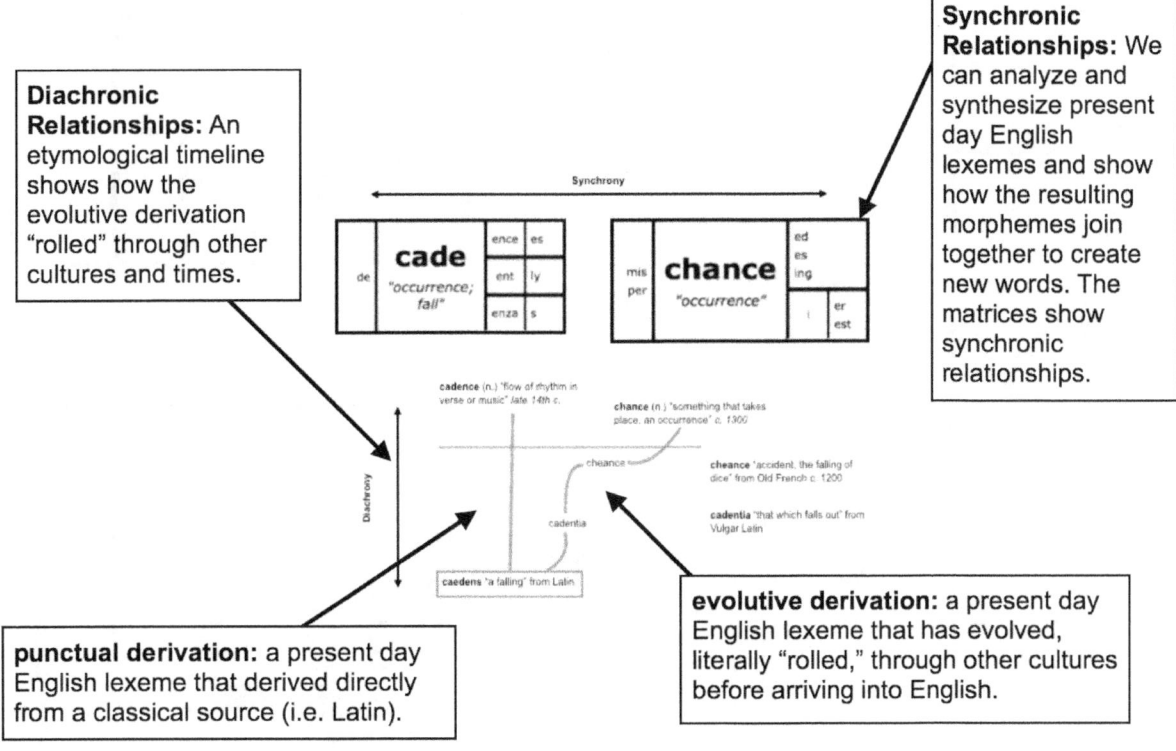

figure 8.1

I have provided three examples of doublets: *fragile ~ frail, legal ~ loyal,* and *cadence ~ chance*, along with generative matrices that can be used to explore more relationships.

For further study: How many other lexical doublets can you discover?

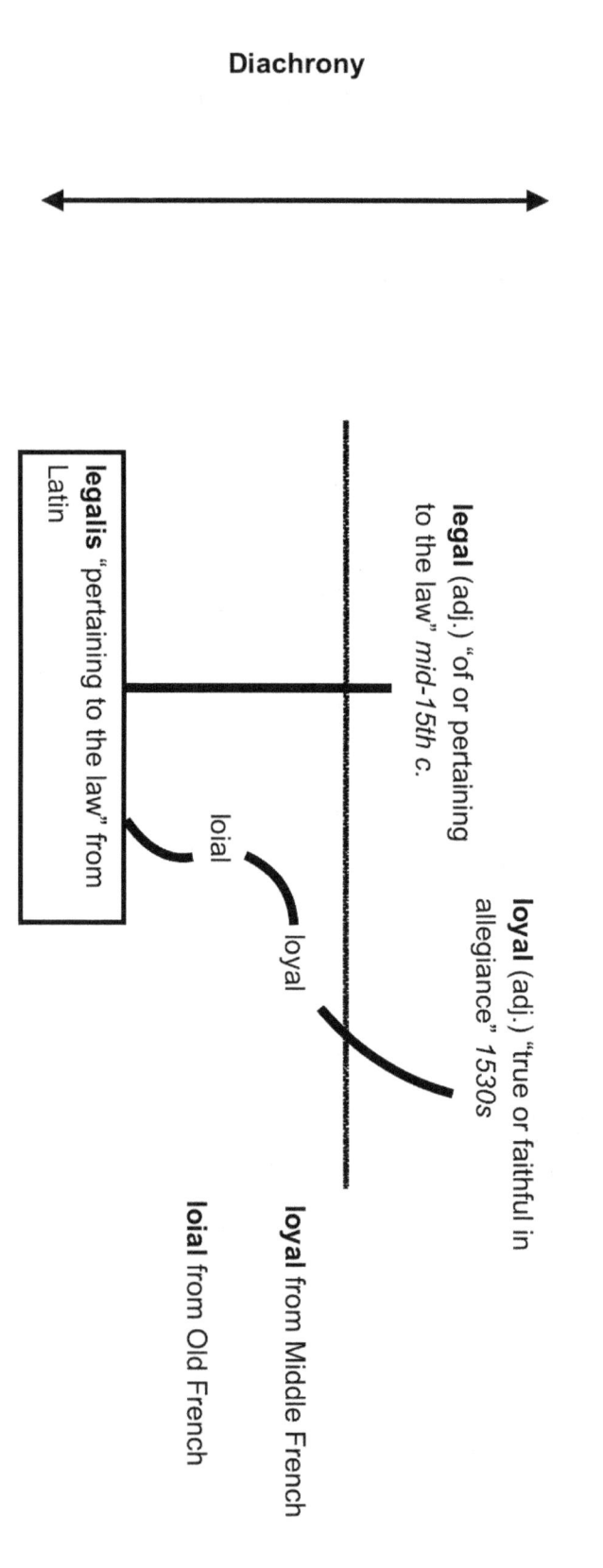
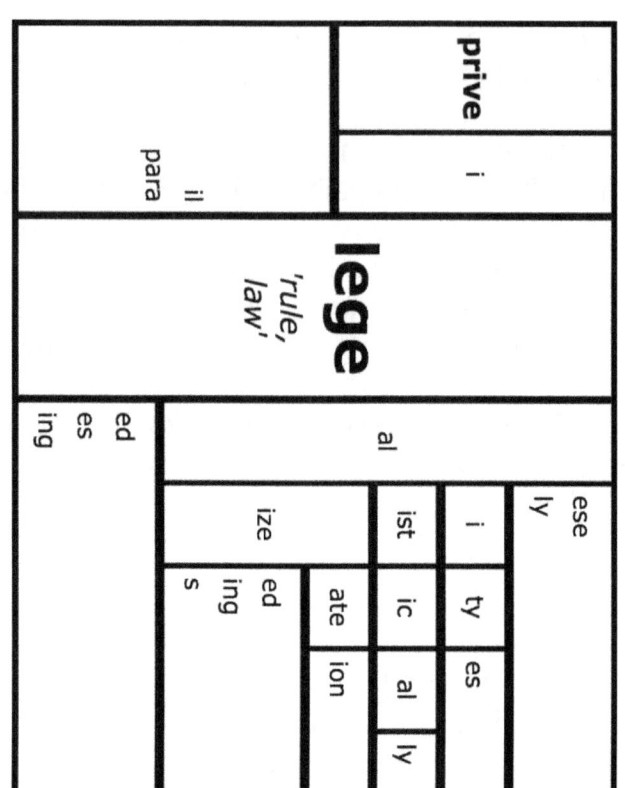
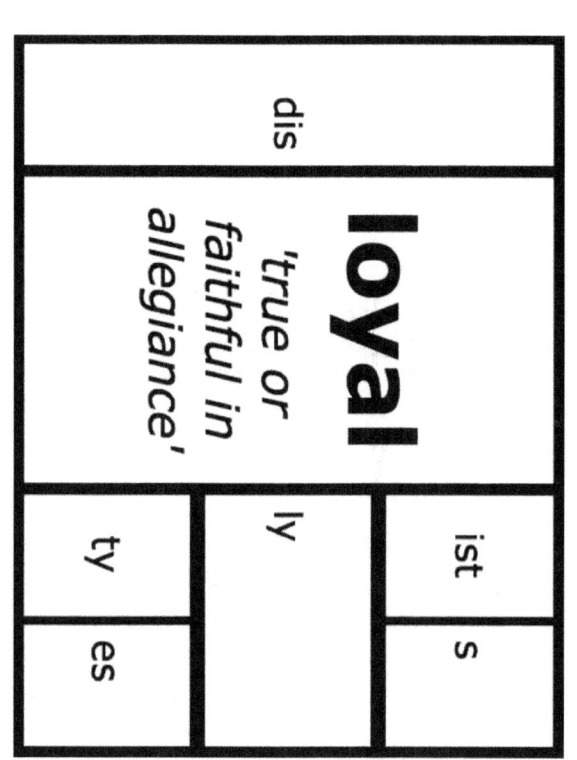

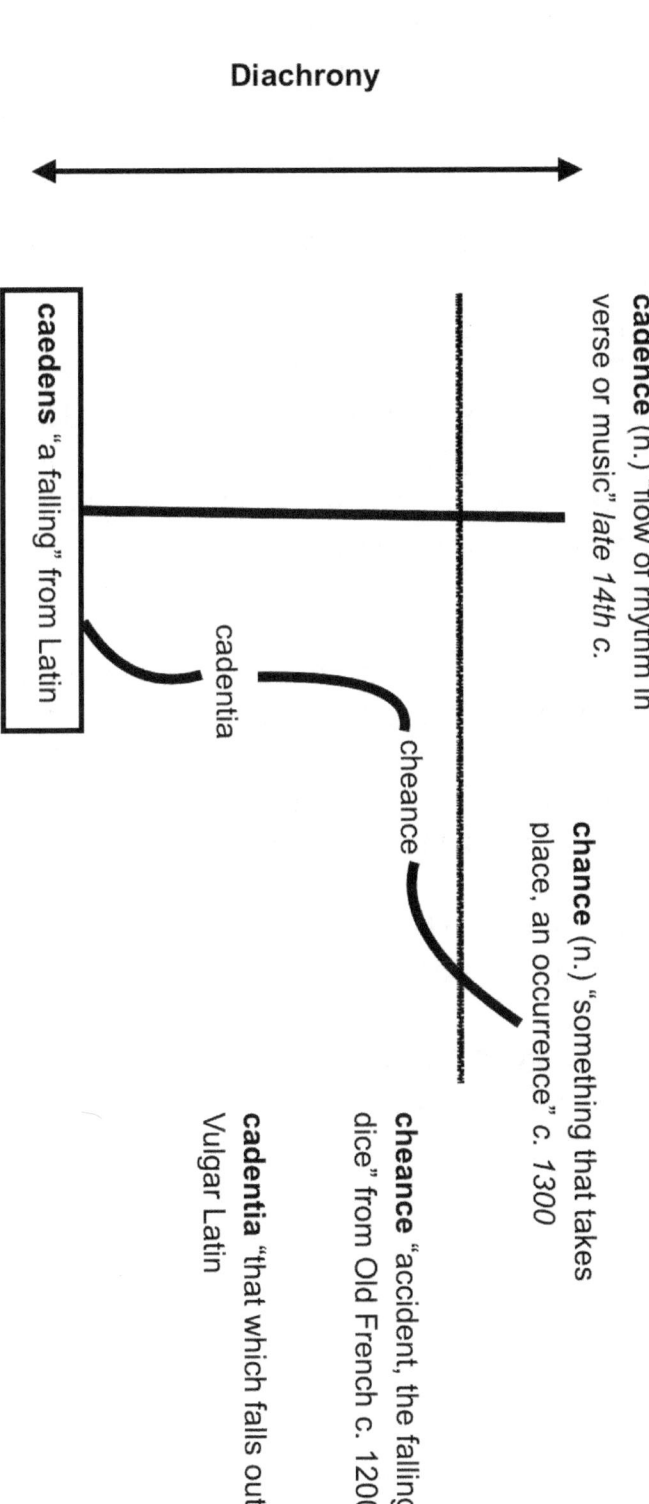
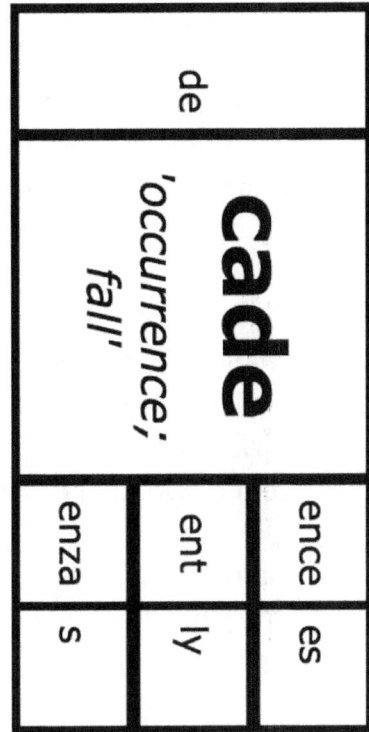

Diachrony / **Synchrony**

caedens "a falling" from Latin

cadentia "that which falls out" from Vulgar Latin

cadentia

cheance

cadence (n.) "flow of rhythm in verse or music" late 14th c.

chance (n.) "something that takes place, an occurrence" c. 1300

cheance "accident, the falling of dice" from Old French c. 1200

Investigating Lexical Doublets reinforces the importance of etymology and the influence of French on the English language.

There is a common misconception that there are layers of language and that Anglo-Saxon (Germanic) words are short everyday words. Latin words are described as multisyllabic (polysyllabic), and Greek is only associated with highly scientific and/or medical terminology.

Evidence dismisses this simplistic view of our language when we consider Latinate words easily found by looking around the classroom: *class, pencil, erase, scissors, glue, student,* and *school* all derive from Latin directly or through French. The French influence, clearly visible in the Lexical Doublets graphics, dispels the idea of a "layers of English" model.

Interestingly, the Anglo-Saxons were a people who primarily spoke Old English. We should be mindful not to confuse a group of people with a language.

Old Norse contributed such words as *gasp, droopy, daze,* and *raft*, among others. Borrowed words from Spanish (*avocado, guacamole, taco*), Japanese (*sake, tempura*), Hindi (*basmati, yoga*) and Native American languages (*moccasin, raccoon*) all contribute to the many cultures represented in English, often each word having a story of its own.

hybrid: a word composed of elements from different languages.

Finally, **hybrids** such as *television, automobile, electrocution, hyperactive,* and *neuroscience* would not fit into a single category or heading.

Lexical Doublets are just one way to introduce students to the influence of other languages on English. There are other types of doublets (e.g. Germanic) that are interesting to explore as well.

Analyzing the Greek Alphabet

The first alphabets came from the Hebrews and Phoenicians, just across the Mediterranean Sea from the Greek civilization. They figured out a way to represent sense and meaning through a symbol system whereby graphemes could represent phonemes. It established orthographic phonology.

Eventually, through exploration and trade, the Greeks received this marvelous new invention. They adapted and adopted the system to meet the needs of their native speakers. The Greeks reassigned letters and added new ones in order to finally replace the complicated syllabary they were previously using.

The Romans, much the way the Greeks did with the Phoenicians, eventually adopted and adapted the alphabet to fit their needs.

This background provides context to the interrelationship of letters between classical languages and how they came into English. It shows that the Greeks were responsible for more than just lending English a few medical or scientific words.

Analyzing Greek lexemes involves the process of transcription, whereby letters from the Greek alphabet are transcribed into Roman letters. There are diacritics (marks around letters) that make the process of transcription complex but highly regular.

The following graphic explores a few relationships between the Greek and Roman alphabets, and provides a few examples of how the Greek alphabet impacts PDE words. There are several other explorations into Greek that are left to the reader to investigate.

Phoenician Alphabet

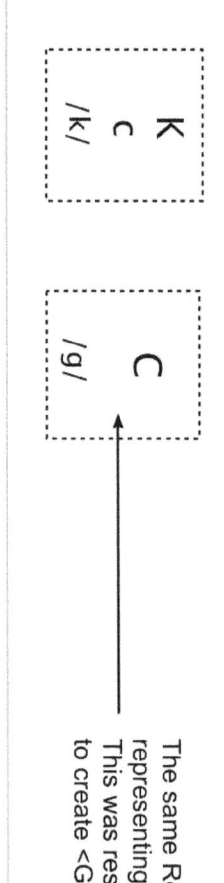

*Arrows signal directionality. Phoenicians, as well as Hebrews, moved from left to right in an 'S' fashion and the Greeks changed it to read left to right.

Greek Alphabet

α	β	γ	δ	ε	ζ	η	θ	ι	κ	λ	μ
a	b	g	d	ĕ	z	ē	th	i	c	l	m

ν	ξ	ο	π	ρ	σ	τ	υ	φ	χ	ψ	ω
n	x	ŏ	p	r	s	t	y	ph	ch	ps	ō

The Greeks had diacritics to signal long and short vowel length. This distinguished meaning between homographs. Vowel length did not signal a different quality of articulation, but actual time. The Romans also had this. What education typically refers to as 'long' and 'short' vowels is actually a misanalysis and the terms should be reserved for referring to duration, not quality.

The breve over the <o> in the Greek omicron signals a short vowel length. The macron over the <o> in the Greek omega signals the same quality articulation, but a longer duration. The same can be applied to Greek epsilon and eta. Omicron is the default connecting vowel letter in Greek.

```
<ŏ>  /a/
 o
```

```
<ō>  /a:/
 ω
```

```
 K      C
 c      /g/
 /k/
```

The same Roman grapheme representing two different phonemes. This was resolved by adding a stroke to create <G> from <C>.

```
 C      G
 /k/    /g/
```

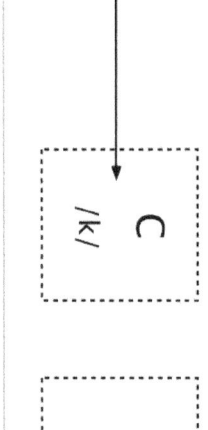

```
 φ
 ph
 /f/
```

<ph> digraph representing /f/ often signals Greek origins:

graph   philosophy   dolphin

```
 χ
 ch
 /k/
```

<ch> digraph representing /k/ often signals Greek origins:

chemistry   alchemy   archaeology

```
 ψ
 ps
 word initial
```

<ps> digraph word initial position often signals Greek origins:

psyche   psalm   pseudonym

What is a blend?

Lewis Carroll's infamous *Jabberwocky* provides a great template for reading lessons. The words are carefully selected to provide the reader with just the right…everything. Carroll incorporates blends with utmost precision, and analyzing his work can be both engaging and rigorous.

The following graphic compares the term *blend* with the currently held definition in education circles. Educators suggest a blend consists of "two or more adjacent consonants or vowels whose sounds flow smoothly together" (Birsh 492). The graphic includes precise definitions for linguistic terms. It distinguishes between descriptors for written language and vocabulary associated with phonology and phonetics.

blends

trans**ceiver**	**trans**mitter	+	**receiver**
fant**abulous**	**fant**astic	+	**abulous** (fabulous)
gin**ormous**	**gi**gantic	+	**ormous** (enormous)
brunch	**br**eakfast	+	l**unch**

A blend has no regards for morphological boundaries, and fragments of words are taken and put together in a variety of ways. From these examples, we see one way a blend is formed. A **juxtaposition** blend is formed from the front part of one word is truncated and positioned with the truncated ending of another word.

There are examples of two other types of blends in Lewis Carroll's *Alice In Wonderland*

galumph
chortle
slithy

For further study:

What types of blends does Lewis Carroll use in his famous poem *Jabberwocky*?

---

clusters
blend - [b], [l]
place - [p], [l]
clump - [c], [l] - [m], [p]

glides
ape - /eɪ/
bite - /aɪ/
pow - /aʊ/
boil - /ɔɪ/

Now that we have a word to define how some English lexemes are formed, we can no longer safely use the word *blend* to describe consonants and/or vowels as they are pronounced. In phonetics, a **cluster** is a sequence of adjacent consonant in the analysis of connected **speech**.

Further, a **glide** is a transition of the vocal chords from one vowel phone to another during

*These are only examples and this is not meant to be an exhaustive list.

clips
taxi
tux
comfy
stereo
sax

Blends are not the same as **clips** -- shortened forms of single lexemes. Nor are blends synonymous with **compounds** or **contractions**.

compounds
mid + night -> midnight
back + yard -> backyard

contractions
isn't -> is not
hasn't -> has not

Precise definitions provide clear terminology to differentiate terminology for written language (blend, clip, compound, contraction) and spoken language (glide, cluster).

Old English Verbs

Old English, a direct ancestor of PDE, is responsible for a number of contributions to spellings. Often dismissed as "irregular" verbs, strong verbs are the remnants of our ancestry.

Analyzing any of the following paradigms provides a deep exploration into patterns that remained for hundreds of years. It is also evidence of how our language changes over time. Consider the PDE verb *leap*. The past tense form could be *leaped* or *leapt*. *Leapt* is the strong form that over time has been weakening, more often taking on the productive suffix <-ed>. Any new verb to PDE (e.g. google) will take the <-ed> suffix. Hence, the weakening process continues. There was even a past participle *lopen*, following the pattern of class VII strong verbs, but it has since fallen out.

Applying knowledge of strong verbs from Old English to the classroom supports student understanding. For example, when a student encounters the word *fell* in context and asks about why there is an <e>, the word can be linked to the present tense *fall* which follows the same pattern as *blow ~ blew* and *know ~ knew*, all deriving from class IV strong verbs in Old English.

For further study, consider the following diachronic spelling changes:

    <sc> ~ <sh>   example: OE: **sc**acan ~ PDE: **sh**aken
    <cn> ~ <kn>   example: OE: **cn**aw ~ PDE: **kn**ow

These are just two examples taken from the paradigms in the graphic, but ample evidence is provided across the language for these relationships. What other examples can you find?

Strong Verbs

The conjugations in Old English reveal consistent patterns in spelling that account for PDE conjugations.

Class I

OE Infinitive	Preterite	Past Participle	PDE Present	Preterite	Past Participle
bītan	bāt	biten	bite	bit	bitten
glīdan	glād	gliden	glide	*glode	*glidden
scīnan	scān	scinen	shine	shone	*shined
drīfan	drāf	drifen	drive	drove	driven

Class II

OE Infinitive	Preterite	Past Participle	PDE Infinitive	Preterite	Past Participle
brēotan	brēat	broten	break	broke	broken
cēosan	cēas	coren	choose	chose	chosen
flēogan	fleag	flogen	fly	flew	flown
crēopan	crēap	cropen	creep	crept	crept

Class III

OE Infinitive	Preterite	Past Participle	PDE Infinitive	Preterite	Past Participle
drincan	dranc	druncen	drink	drank	drunk
scrincan	scranc	scruncen	shrink	shrank	shrunk
singan	sang	sungen	sing	sang	sung
swimman	swamm	swummen	swim	swam	swum

Class IV

OE Infinitive	Preterite	Past Participle	PDE Infinitive	Preterite	Past Participle
beran	bær	boren	bear	bore	borne
brecan	bræc	brocen	break	broke	broken
stelan	stælc	stolcen	steal	stole	stolen
cuman	cōm	cumen	come	came	*comen

Class V

OE Infinitive	Preterite	Past Participle	PDE Infinitive	Preterite	Past Participle
etan	æt	eten	eat	ate	eaten
specan	spræc	sprecen	speak	spoke	spoken
wefan	wæf	wefen	weave	wove	woven
giefan	geaf	giefen	give	gave	given

Class VI

OE Infinitive	Preterite	Past Participle	PDE Infinitive	Preterite	Past Participle
dragan	drōg	dragen	draw	drew	drawn
scacan	scōc	scacen	shake	shook	shaken
standan	stōd	standen	stand	stood	stood

Class VII

OE Infinitive	Preterite	Past Participle	PDE Infinitive	Preterite	Past Participle
cnāwan	cnēow	cnāwn	know	knew	known
blāwan	blēow	blāwen	blow	blew	blown
feallan	fēoll	feallen	fall	fell	fallen
hlēapan	hlēop	hlēapen	leap	*leapt	*lopen

*Some forms have "weakened" over time, taking the Present-Day English <-ed> productive past tense suffix. Other forms have fallen out completely.

Grimm's Law

The following graphic is rooted in Grimm's Law. He compared multiple languages and noticed that initial consonants from PIE went through changes as they evolved into Classic languages (Greek and Latin) and Germanic (Old English, Old Norse) languages. The graphic illustrates three of those changes.

PDE words derive from both Germanic and Classic languages, sometimes from the same PIE reconstructed root. In the etymology diagram, we see that the English word *percent* with an initial /p/ derives from Latin and *hundred* with initial /h/ derives from Old English.

Any of the word pairs offered are interesting investigations on their own.

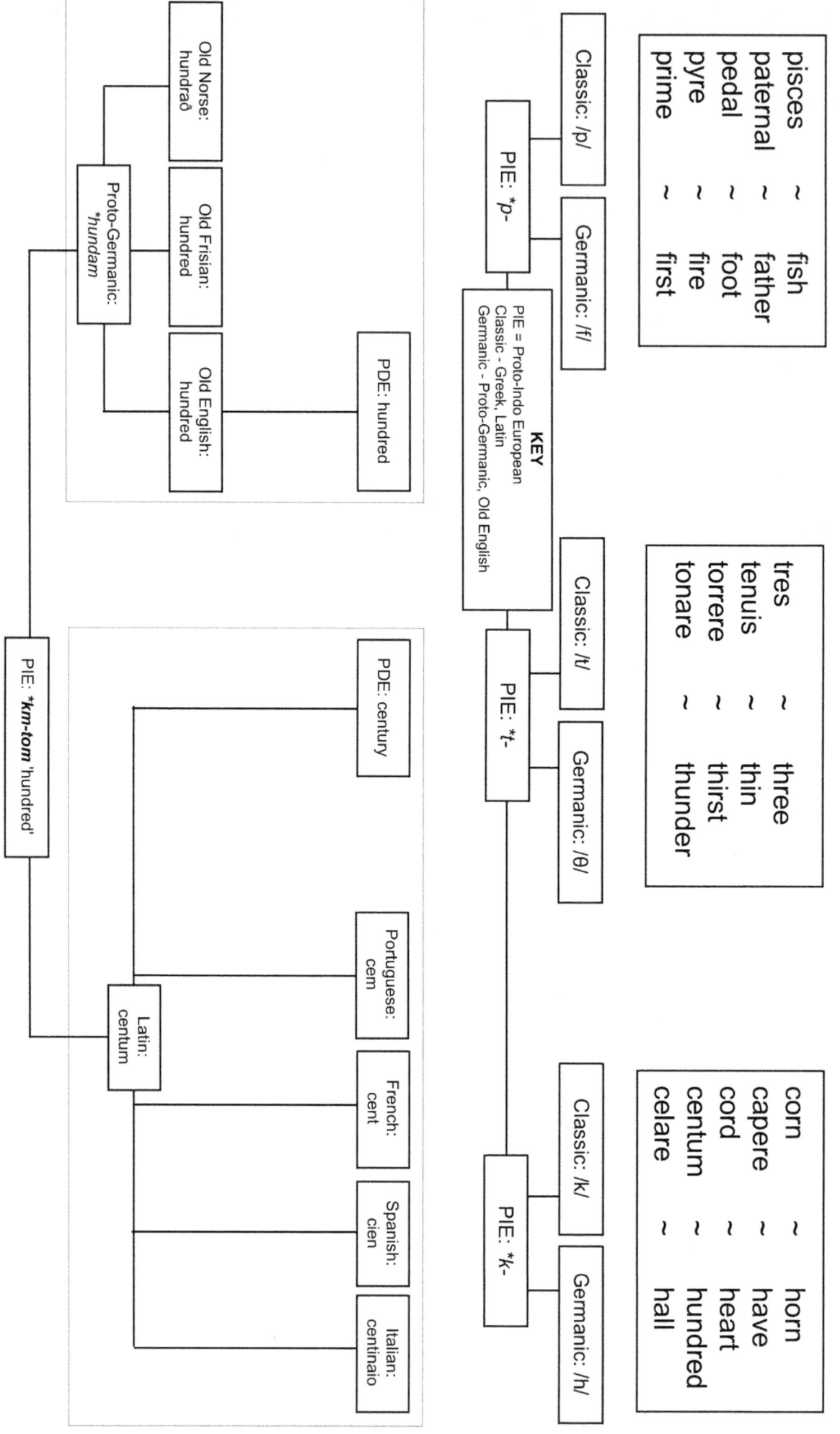

Integrating Content

Up to this point, the focus has been on analyzing words through language structures. Most of the graphics are designed from a "word first" perspective, meaning that lists of words in the graphics were created to show deeper patterns within the language itself. However, the historical context, when analyzing words scientifically, is often missing. Take, for example, the word camera. If we look at an etymology chart of the word, and add an approximate vertical timeline, we can make an interesting discovery:

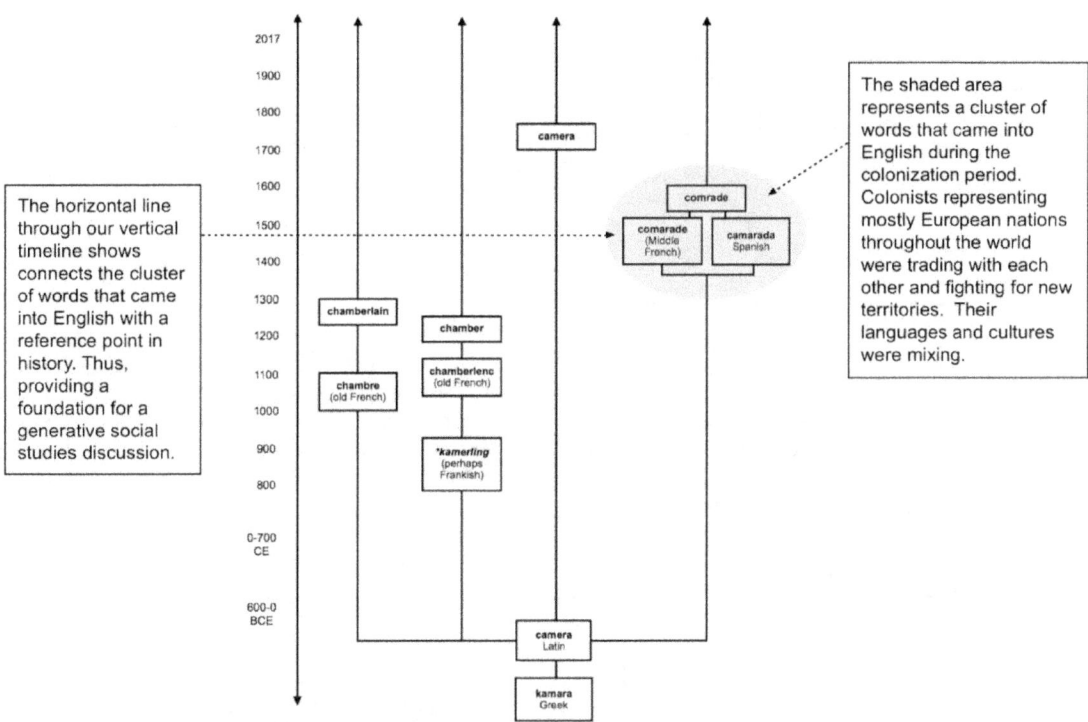

figure 9.1

The vertical timeline is consistent with how I explore diachronic relationships with my students, but that doesn't always have to be the case. A horizontal timeline is commonly used in textbooks.

When investigating the orthography of a list of words that came into English during World War II, my students made some interesting discoveries. The graphic on the following page was made from an analysis of the word *paratroops*. A possible connection between *troop* and *tavern* can lead to a discussion about dissimilation. An analysis revealing the morphemes: *paratroops -> para + troop + s* and subsequent search for etymology leads to the discovery that *para-* comes from Greek and, in this particular word, is a clip of *parachute*. *Chute* is a free base that derives from French, ultimately from Latin *cadere*. Other words on the timeline that merit further study include *blockbuster, weimaraner,* and *walkie-talkie*.

Applying word analysis skills to math, science, art and music provides instructional value in content classes as well. For example, analyzing the words for the days of the week connects the calendar, astronomy, and the Germanic and Classic languages. In addition, by comparing multiple languages, we can determine how words came to be spelled regularly in English.

One example is *Wednesday,* named after Woden, the Germanic God of Speed, that has a direct parallel with *miércoles,* the Spanish word for Wednesday. *Miércoles* is named after the Roman God of Speed, Mercury.

Figure 9.2 is one example that outlines this relationship. Notice the similarity in spellings of the words in Spanish, French, and Italian. It is contrasted with the similarities between the spellings in Old English, Old Frisian, and Old Norse. This is evidence of cultural differences between civilizations and the words used to celebrate those cultures.

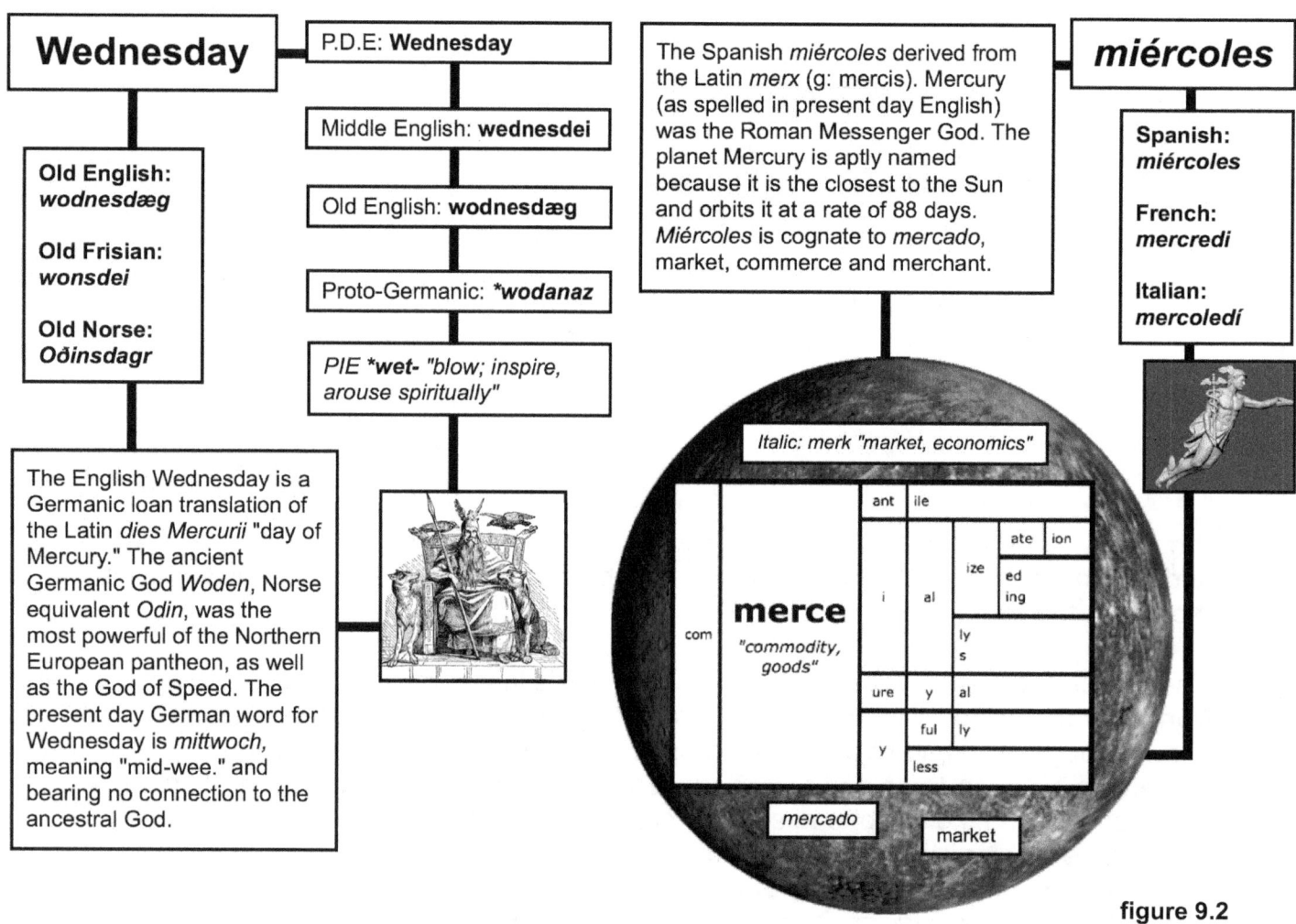

figure 9.2

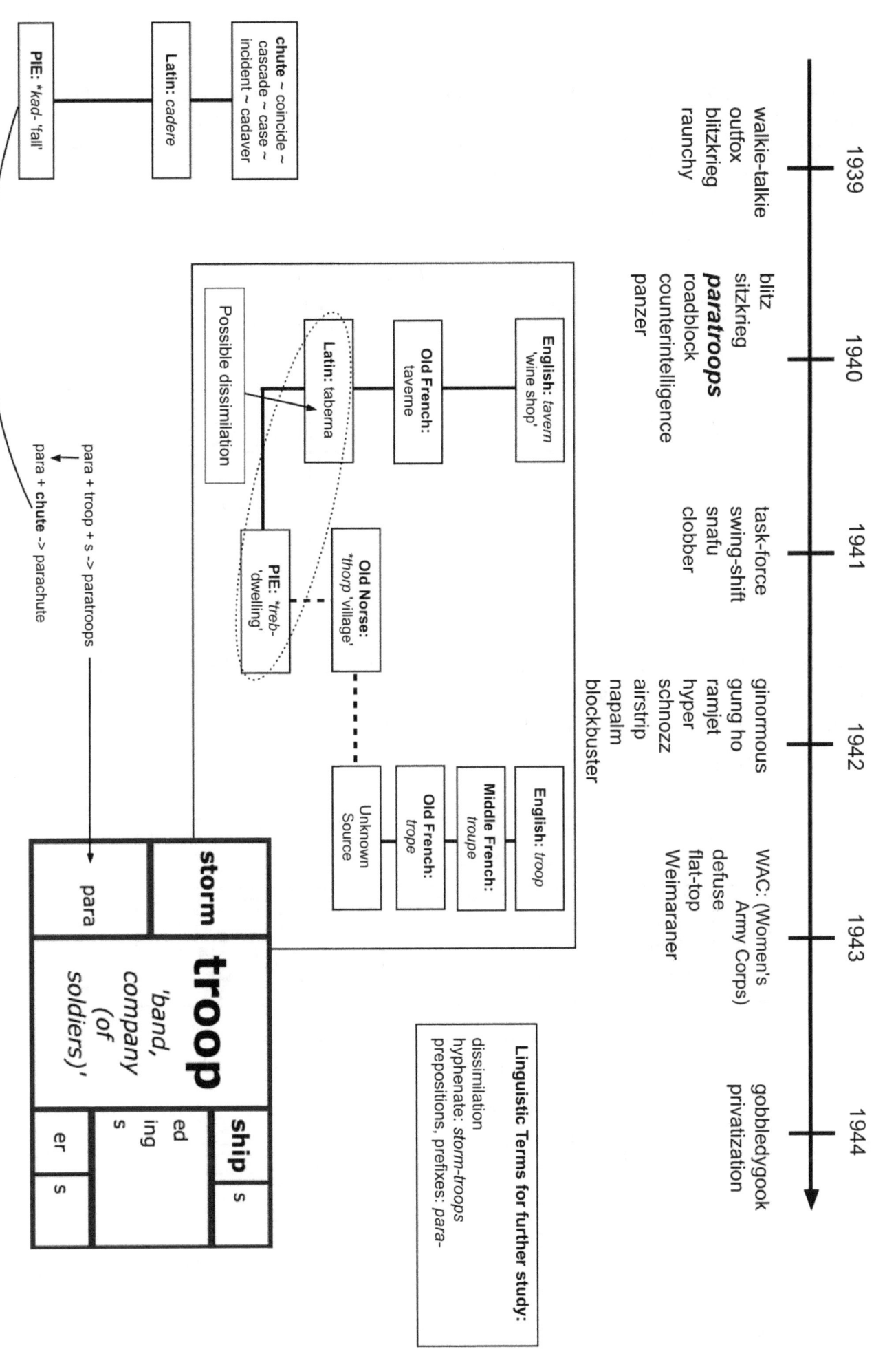

Likewise, analyzing words representing cardinal numbers provides a strong foundation to concepts that might otherwise be overlooked. One example is the word *eight* containing the <igh> trigraph, often cognate to the Latinate <ct>. *Night ~ nocturnal* and *eight ~ October* are just two examples.

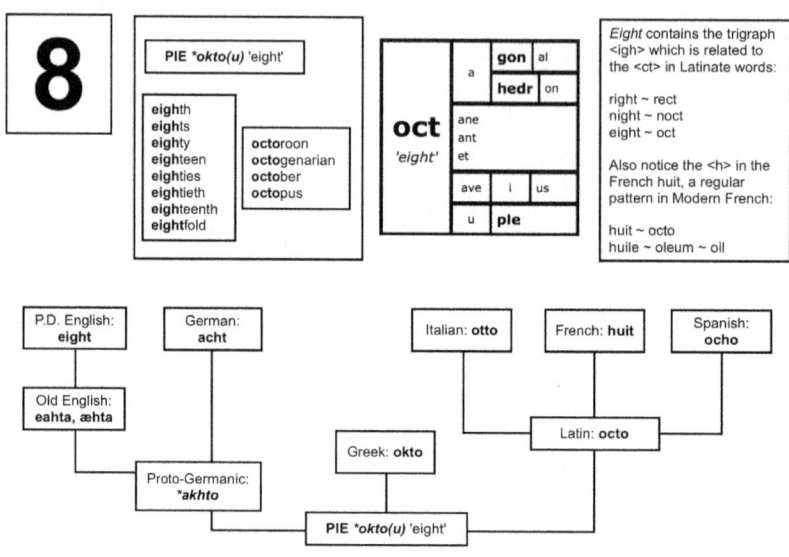

figure 9.3

Investigating math vocabulary is another way to reinforce vocabulary while also connecting words and language to the content areas. In figure 9.4, the word *multiply* is analyzed and the resulting elements can be connected with social studies, math, reading, and art.

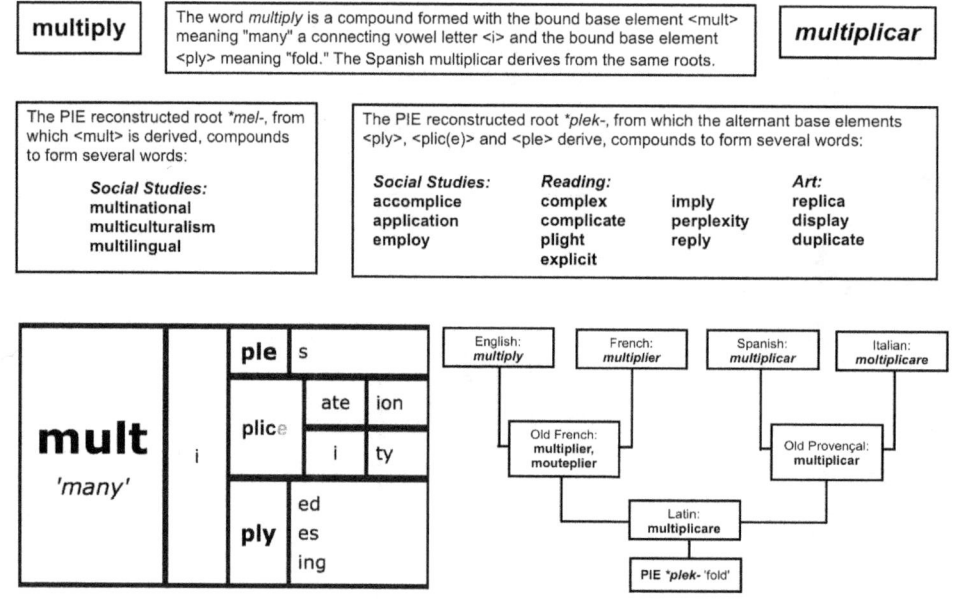

figure 9.4

Conclusion

The descriptions and graphics included in this book were designed to give educators the scaffolding to help support instruction in orthographic linguistics. Despite the depth of knowledge covered, there are many aspects of our language that are not explored: grammar, fluency, comprehension, supralexical structures, executive functions, psychological and cognitive science, to name a few.

Analyzing the written word is one part of literacy instruction that can be integrated with other pieces within a language arts lesson. The more the teacher knows about how our orthography works, the better equipped they are to respond to student inquiries.

My hope is that these graphics will prompt further inquiry and investigation using scientific principles as a guide for exploration of the structures of English orthography.

References

Birsh, J. R. (2002). *Multisensory teaching of basic language skills.* Baltimore, MD: P.H. Brookes Pub. Co.

Carroll, L., & Gardner, M. (1965). *The Annotated Alice: Alice's Adventures in Wonderland and Through the Looking Glass.* Harmondsworth, Middlesex.

Crystal, D., & Crystal, D. (2008). *Dictionary of Linguistics and Phonetics.* Malden, MA: Blackwell Publishing.

Henry, Marcia Kierland. *Unlocking literacy: effective decoding & spelling instruction.* Paul H. Brookes, 2010.

Mitchell, Bruce, and Fred C. Robinson. *A guide to old English.* John Wiley & Sons, 2012.

"IPA Chart, http://www.internationalphoneticassociation.org/content/ipa-chart, available under a Creative Commons Attribution-Sharealike 3.0 Unported License. Copyright © 2015 International Phonetic Association."

"Linguist Educator Exchange." *LEX*, www.linguisteducatorexchange.com/.

"Online Etymology Dictionary." *Online Etymology Dictionary*, www.etymonline.com/.

"The Oxford English Dictionary." *Oxford Dictionaries*, Oxford Dictionaries, www.oxforddictionaries.com/oed.

"Real Spelling." www.realspelling.fr/.

"Word Works Kingston." www.wordworkskingston.com/.

www.ingramcontent.com/pod-product-compliance
Lightning Source LLC
Chambersburg PA
CBHW060420300426
44111CB00018B/2923